Applied Computer Science

Shane Torbert

Applied Computer Science

Second Edition

 Springer

Shane Torbert
Fairfax, Virginia, USA

ISBN 978-3-319-80902-1   ISBN 978-3-319-30866-1   (eBook)
DOI 10.1007/978-3-319-30866-1

This Springer imprint is published by Springer Nature
The registered company is Springer International Publishing AG Switzerland

For my wife

I don't believe that talent belongs to a certain place... it's spread equally. The problem is, in very few places we create conditions to help this talent to be discovered and nurtured.
  –Garry Kasparov

Preface

Efforts to increase student participation in computing, at both the high school and undergraduate levels, have taken a bizarre turn. More accurately, my own perception of the motivation of activists has clarified and, embarrassingly, I can't believe what I'm seeing.

Why has a desire to identify previously unidentified talent in under-represented demographic groups now morphed into a search for some small set of minimal work that can be "accomplished" by all students? How is something-for-everyone going to inspire the best-among-us to unleash their hidden creativities? Do serious people think such a strategy could benefit anyone who was not already entrenched?

There *is* talent for computing in black students, in girls, and among poor people. Not in everyone, any more than all white males or well-off Asians, most of whom have no computing abilities whatsoever despite "their" dominance of the industry, but a significant and representative amount. We need to activate these groups.

All talents are spread equally. Computing students are out there. *Find them.* Encourage, prepare and challenge them. Nurture this ability as you would a champion. But if you cannot bring yourself to act like you really believe they can do it then please, leave them alone. But don't deceive them.

Annandale, Virginia   Shane Torbert
April 2015

Contents

Chapter 1
Simulation

Experiments are often limited by a high level of danger, and because they are too expensive or simply impossible to arrange, such as in developing new medical treatments, vehicles for space flight, and also studying geologic events. In these cases we may benefit from the use of computer simulation to refine our understanding and narrow our investigation prior to an "official" observation. Since the promise of this technique is to accelerate information gathering for a relatively low total cost, interest has been gaining momentum *everywhere*.

Examples in this chapter include discrete, continuous, and interactive systems with particular importance given to the long-term (asymptotic) trend as the scale of a problem grows toward infinity. Our approach favors clarity and context over trivia or theory with the hope that this better enables early success, but of course in learning there are never any real guarantees. Efficiency matters but is not paramount as we prefer to implement more widely accessible solutions while perhaps merely suggesting a state-of-the-art method.

For all code listings we use Python 2 with Tk and PIL, plus gnuplot, but other options are available (e.g., Matlab®, *Mathematica*, Python 3, Java, C/C++, Fortran, Scheme, Pascal) and our belief is these choices are sufficiently intuitive to serve as instructive pseudocode, that also happens to run!, for any environment you use. Regardless, we feel the central issues up-front are quality problems, a thoughtful sequencing of topics, and rapid feedback.

1.1 Random Walk

Imagine yourself outside on a pleasant day looking for a nice place to sit and read. By chance you are standing exactly halfway between your two favorite spots but are unable to decide which one to take. Out of curiosity you engage in a rather obscure process to settle the matter: you flip a coin and take one step in the indicated direction, then flip again followed by another step, and again and again, moving back-and-forth as the coin dictates, possibly coming very close to one spot or the

© Springer International Publishing 2016

S. Torbert, *Applied Computer Science*, DOI 10.1007/978-3-319-30866-1_1

Table 1.1: Three examples of a size $n = 5$ random walk

```
-----X-----          -----X-----          -----X-----
----X|-----          -----|X----          -----|X----
-----X-----          -----|-X---          -----|-X---
----X|-----          -----|X----          -----|X----
---X--|-----         -----X-----          -----X-----
--X--|-----          ----X|-----          -----|X----
-X---|-----          ---X-|-----          -----|-X---
--X--|-----          ----X|-----          -----|--X--
-X---|-----          -----X-----          -----|-X---
--X--|-----          ----X|-----          -----|--X--
---X-|-----          ---X-|-----          -----|-X---
--X--|-----          --X--|-----          -----|X----
-X---|-----          -X---|-----          -----|-X---
X----|-----          --X--|-----          -----|--X--
-----|-----          -X---|-----          -----|---X-
Steps:   14          X----|-----          -----|----X
                     -X---|-----          -----|-----
                     X----|-----          Steps:   16
                     -----|-----
                     Steps:   18
```

other but ending only when a final step brings you all the way there. We wish to simulate this random drifting process with computer code. Each lab is numbered so that the first digit indicates chapter (1–8), the second a particular problem (1–3) in the chapter, and the third digit your specific assignment (1–5) related to the problem.

Lab111: Trace of a Single Run

We begin with output as shown in Table 1.1 where variables specify the size of our walk and also track current position. If n is the distance from the halfway point to the edge just next to either destination then $m = 2n + 1$ is the total distance available for drifting.

Code Listing 1.1: Initializing variables

```
#
n=5
m=2*n+1
j=  n+1
#
```

The values of n and m remain constant here but our current position j will start at the halfway point $j = n + 1$ and then change as we drift until either $j = 0$ or $j = m + 1$ and we have arrived at a reading spot. Whenever $j = 1$ or $j = m$ we are at one of the two edges, needing but a single step more in that direction to complete our walk. Commands to initialize and update these variables "over time" are shown in Code Listings 1.1 and 1.2, respectively.

Code Listing 1.2: A complete walk's loop

```
while 1<=j<=m:
    #
    if random()<0.5: # coin flip
        j+=1
    else:
        j-=1
    #
```

Of course we want to *see* the walk, too. Once we know everything is working properly this "trace" will be less important but we should first verify that our code is behaving as expected. We could just print the value of j at each step but it will be better if we draw a "picture" instead. Helper variable k loops over the entire drifting area in Code Listing 1.3 to display a single row from any of Table 1.1's examples.

Code Listing 1.3: A loop to display the entire drifting area

```
k=1
while k<=m:
    if k==j:
        print 'X',        # current position
    elif k==n+1:
        print '|',        # halfway point
    else:
        print '-',
    k+=1
print
```

Your first assignment is to put all this code together into a 1-D random walk simulation, including counting-up the total number of steps.

Questions to consider:

- Do our examples represent a typical size $n = 5$ random walk?
- What happens to the number of steps, on average, as n increases?

Fig. 1.1: Law of large numbers applied to coin flips

Lab112: Law of Large Numbers

Before proceeding we ask an essential question: After how many coin flips are we reasonably sure the heads-tails ratio is "close" to even? Your assignment is to write a small program that only flips coins, over and over and over again, to calculate the percentage of heads, or tails, obtained. Code Listing 1.4 is a sample gnuplot script for a plot similar to the one shown in Fig. 1.1, where we assume the program's output (total observed probability after each trial) has been stored in a plain text file.

Code Listing 1.4: Sample gnuplot script

```
set terminal png
set output "lab112.png"
set title  "Coin Flip Results"
set ylabel "Observed Probability"
set yrange[0.45:0.55]
set ytics 0.01
plot "lab112.txt" with lines notitle,0.505 w l notitle
```

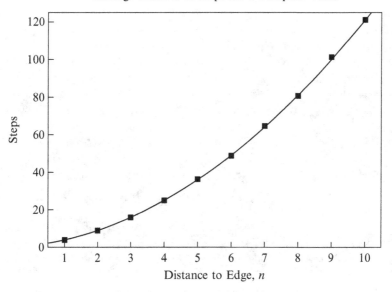

Fig. 1.2: Quadratic growth in the average number of steps to complete a walk

Lab113: Scaling the Problem Size

We show the average number of steps for walks of size $n \leq 10$ in Fig. 1.2 overlaid with the curve $f(n) = (n+1)^2$ since it takes $n+1$ total steps in a particular direction to actually end the walk. A trial now is an entire random walk, not just a single coin flip, and we use Algorithm 1.1.1 and 10,000 trials for accurate results.

Algorithm 1.1.1 Average number of steps for various n

 1: **while** $n \leq n_{max}$ **do**
 2:   $steps = 0$
 3:   **while** $t = 1 \rightarrow trials$ **do**
 4:     **while** $random\_walk$ **do**
 5:       $\ldots$
 6:       $steps = steps + 1$
 7:     **end while**
 8:   **end while**
 9:   **print** $n, steps/trials$
10: **end while**

Fig. 1.3: A large plume of ash during an eruption of the Mt. Cleveland volcano, Alaska, as seen from the International Space Station on 23 May 2006 (Image courtesy of the Image Science and Analysis Laboratory, NASA Johnson Space Center)

Transport and Diffusion

Observation of the physical world often reveals behavior that may be explained at least partially by drifting. For instance, the plume of ash shown in Fig. 1.3 moves in two fundamental ways. First, wind blows the ash in some direction, a topic we will consider in more detail with the next problem. Second, the ash spreads out and eventually the plume will break-up in a process called *diffusion* that can be modeled by the random motion of individual ash particles. This means that our random walk, while an absurd method for picking a spot to read, does relate accurately to the diffusive aspect of a plume's movement over time.

However, volcanic eruptions may have a worldwide impact over many years, scales far too large for 3-D particle-by-particle calculations even for state of the art algorithms running night and day on the fastest computers in the world. Simulations of such cases require a team of experts (we need you!) to build different models, better algorithms, and bigger computers.

See also *Assessing Maximum Possible Damage for Contaminant Release Events* by Fernando Camelli and Rainald Löhner, from the George Mason University School of Computational Sciences.

Fig. 1.4: Blue Mountain supercomputer, Los Alamos National Laboratory, New Mexico, one of the most powerful computing systems in the world at the end of the twentieth century (Image courtesy of Los Alamos National Security, LLC)

Parallel Processing

One popular technique for large-scale simulations is the use of multiple systems connected together to process sub-units of the overall code in parallel. For instance, individual trials in the previous lab are independent of each other and therefore may be run simultaneously on separate machines in order to speed up calculation.

The parallel computing system shown in Fig. 1.4 was one of the world's most powerful supercomputers. It has since been decommissioned and not even a decade later the same level of capability became commercially available in graphics cards, also massively parallel but no longer the exclusive domain of a premier national lab the use of whose image requires:

Unless otherwise indicated, this information has been authored by an employee or employees of the Los Alamos National Security, LLC (LANS), operator of the Los Alamos National Laboratory under Contract No. DE-AC52-06NA25396 with the U.S. Department of Energy. The U.S. Government has rights to use, reproduce, and distribute this information. The public may copy and use this information without charge, provided that this Notice and any statement of authorship are reproduced on all copies. Neither the Government nor LANS makes any warranty, express or implied, or assumes any liability or responsibility for the use of this information.

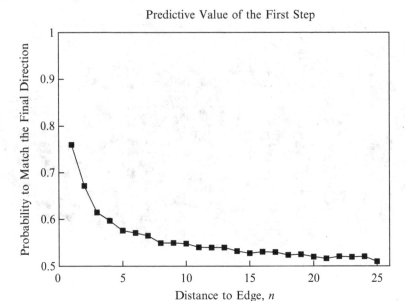

Fig. 1.5: As the size of the walk increases the importance of the first step decreases

Lab114: Predictive Value of the First Step

We want to know how important the first step is in determining the final direction our drifting leads. Code Listing 1.5 shows how the first step can be "remembered" for later comparison after the entire walk has finished. Your job is to count the number of times this very first step matches the final direction. Results for $n \leq 25$ shown in Fig. 1.5 reflect again the use of 10,000 trials for each size.

Code Listing 1.5: Remembering the first step for later comparison

```
j=n+1
if random()<0.5:
    j+=1
else:
    j-=1
first_step=(j-(n+1)) # either 1 or -1
#
while 1<=j<=m:
    #
    ...
```

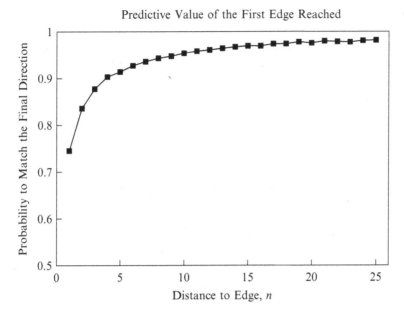

Fig. 1.6: The importance of the first edge reached increases with the size of the walk

Lab115: Predictive Value of the First Edge Reached

Asking a similar question about the first edge allows us to use the symmetry of our problem to speed up runtime. It is not necessary to start in the middle and wait for the drifting to eventually reach an edge; instead, just start on an edge at step one! Results for $n \leq 25$ shown in Fig. 1.6 are consistent regardless of which edge we start on and again reflect the use of 10,000 trials for each size.

Code Listing 1.6: Using symmetry to speed up a first edge calculation

```
j=m
#
while 1<=j<=m:  # walk starts at edge
    #
    ...
    #
#
if j==m+1:        # was there a match ?
    #
    ...
```

Probability

Let P_i be the probability of ending a walk at $j = m+1$ after having started the walk at $j = n+1+i$. So $P_0 = 0.5$ and $P_{n+1} = 1$. Lab114 and Lab115 suggest:

$$P_1 = 0.5 + \frac{0.5}{n+1}$$

$$P_n = 1.0 - \frac{0.5}{n+1}$$

which follow from the fact that P_i grows linearly as i increases from 0 to $n+1$.

Since the coin is fair, our next position after starting the walk is either one step left or one step right, with equal probability:

$$P_i = \frac{P_{i-1}}{2} + \frac{P_{i+1}}{2}$$

Clearing denominators:

$$2P_i = P_{i-1} + P_{i+1}$$

Re-arranging terms:

$$P_i - P_{i-1} = P_{i+1} - P_i = \Delta P$$

The change ΔP is constant and we say P grows *linearly* with respect to i. There are $n+1$ incremental changes from $i = 0$ to $n+1$ and a total change in P of 0.5, therefore each incremental change is:

$$\Delta P = \frac{0.5}{n+1}$$

and the results for P_1 and P_n are confirmed. Code Listing 1.7 and Fig. 1.7 show the case $n = 9$, in context.

Code Listing 1.7: Calculating the predictive value of a starting displacement

```
while i<=n:         # starting displacement
   #
   j=n+1+i
   #
   while 1<=j<=m: # random walk
      #
      ...
      #
   #
   if j==m+1:      # was there a match ?
      #
      ...
```

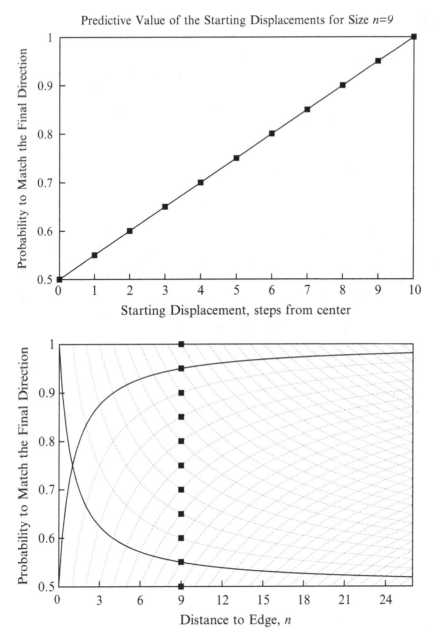

Fig. 1.7: Starting displacements of a size $n = 9$ random walk. *Top*: linear change in probability, from $P = 0.5$ to $P = 1$. *Bottom*: The same probabilities highlighted within the family of all displacements up to size $n = 25$. Also highlighted are the first step and first edge probabilities previously investigated in Lab114 and Lab115

1.2 Air Resistance

Imagine some friends in a sunny field kicking the soccer ball around. If the ball leaves your foot at 60 miles per hour and forming a 30 degree angle with the ground then how far does it go? What does its trajectory look like? Such questions are often asked in math and science classrooms* but our investigation will approach this problem from the standpoint of computer simulation.

Lab121: Deconstructed Parabola

We begin by neglecting air resistance but it will be clear that, using our approach, including air resistance in the model is straightforward. In all cases we restrict ourselves to 2-D and some behavior, such as lift and spin, will not be considered.

The soccer ball's velocity and position are initialized in Code Listing 1.8 where we assume $v_0 = 26.82$ meters per second and $\theta = \pi/6$ radians have already been converted from mph and degrees, and cos and sin are imported from math.

Our main loop shown in Code Listing 1.9 updates the position (x,y) based on the velocity (v_x, v_y) with v_x constant (for now) and v_y itself updated by the "pull" of gravity, $g = -9.81$ m/s^2 near the surface of the Earth.

Code Listing 1.8: Initializing variables

```
#
vx=v0*cos(theta)
vy=v0*sin(theta)
#
x=0.0
y=0.0
```

Code Listing 1.9: A complete trajectory's loop

```
#
while y>=0.0:
    #
    x+=(vx*dt)
    y+=(vy*dt)
    #
    vy+=(g*dt)
    #
```

---

* See, for instance: R. Larson et al., *Algebra 2*. McDougal Littell, 2004.

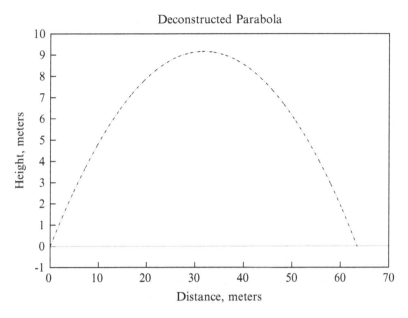

Fig. 1.8: Trajectory plot without air resistance

Obviously v_y changes since what goes up must come down. We can think of v_x as a non-diffusive "transport" similar to the previously unexamined aspect of the ash plume's motion. We use a timestep $dt = 0.001$ seconds and total time t can also be tracked. If our loop outputs (t, x, y) at each step then Code Listing 1.10 plots the overall (x, y) trajectory as shown in Fig. 1.8.

Code Listing 1.10: Trajectory gnuplot script

```
set terminal png
set output "lab121.png"
set title  "Deconstructed Parabola"
set xtics nomirror
plot "lab121.txt" using 2:3 w l notitle,0 w l notitle
```

Two observations about a soccer ball's motion make this simulation possible:

• Horizontal and vertical movement can be treated separately.
• Small enough timesteps allow for straightforward modeling.

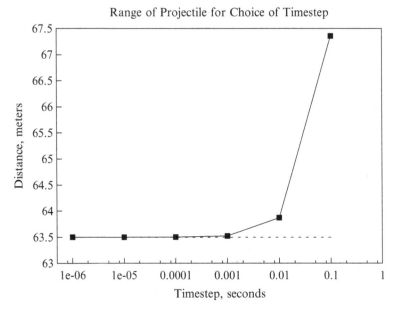

Fig. 1.9: Logarithmic scale for x with `set logscale x` in gnuplot

Lab122: Timestep Study

The range of a projectile is horizontal distance traveled before impact; a test of timesteps for the soccer ball range is shown in Fig. 1.9 with $dt = 10^{-N}$ and $N \leq 6$. Our results indicate $dt = 0.001$ is a good compromise (if $dt = 0.0001$ then our main loop would require 10 times the number of steps). Some anticipated objections:

- Use the exact formula $y = gt^2/2 + v_0 \sin(\theta)t + y_0$ instead of simulation.

  - First, with air resistance the exact formula will be more complicated to derive.
  - Second, our Fig. 1.8 had the simulation and "exact" values in two different dash-patterns and yet they overlaid so well as to seem like only one, not two.

- Our choice of $dt = 0.001$ seconds gives an incorrect range.

  - It is hard to say precisely what is the correct range. Did the ball leave your foot at 60 mph or was it really 61 mph? Was the angle 30° or 29°?

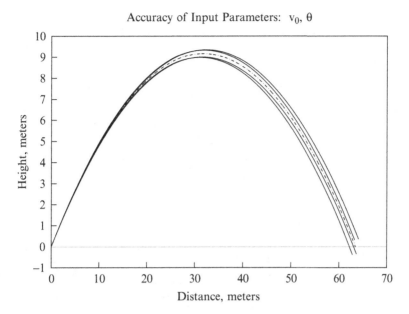

Fig. 1.10: Variation in trajectory for a 1 % change in each input parameter

To elaborate on this, Fig. 1.10 shows the variation in trajectory corresponding to a 1 % change in each input parameter, using the exact formula. Results are closer when only the angle changes but still the two dashed curves clearly coincide best. Even comparing the range to its exact value $x = v_0^2 \sin(2\theta)/|g|$, the horizontal line from Fig. 1.9, our simulation with $dt = 0.001$ seconds is accurate to within one-tenth of one percent.

Lab123: Physical Model

Since the simulation is now working we wish to augment our model $a_x = 0$, $a_y = g$ with terms that reflect air resistance. Code Listing 1.11 shows how this might look.

Code Listing 1.11: Acceleration that varies with velocity

```
#
ax=(  -c1*vx)
ay=(g-c1*vy)
#
```

Fig. 1.11: Trajectory plot with air resistance

A better model for air resistance is $a = -c_1 v - c_2 v^2$ but the quadratic term is more complicated in 2-D and our focus here is foremost on the "big idea" and how it appears in your code. Namely, the idea is that air resistance opposes the direction of motion (hence the minus sign) and also scales with increased speed.

Our plots reflect $c_1 = 0.5$, an ad hoc value, where in general this would depend on the material property of the projectile, its shape, the composition of air, current altitude, etc. The mass is also an implicit part of the c_1 coefficient.

Note the dramatic changes in both height and range compared to our parabolic trajectory; if this seems too unreasonable you should change c_1. (After all, it is your code.) Disclaimer: Any similarities to an actual product or scenario-of-interest is unintentional and must occur purely by chance.

Code Listing 1.12: Fix the x-axis in place for comparing multiple plots

```
set terminal png
set output "lab124.png"
set xrange[:35]
plot "lab124.txt" u 2:3 w l notitle,0 w l notitle
```

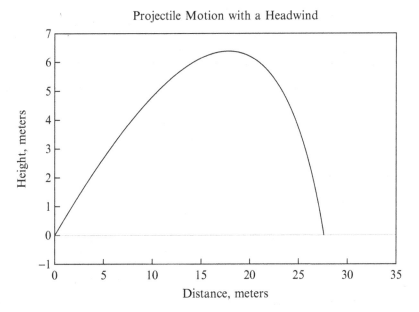

Fig. 1.12: Trajectory plot with air resistance and a headwind of 10 mph

Lab124: Wind

Code Listing 1.12 shows a script that fixes the x-axis in place for comparison of multiple plots. If we assume there is a horizontal wind only and call v_w its velocity then we can model this wind by calculating the relative velocity $(v_x - v_w)$ as shown in Code Listing 1.13. We use relative velocity instead of the absolute v_x to determine the horizontal acceleration due to air resistance.

Since v_y is not affected by v_w the calculation of a_y is exactly as it was before and comparing Figs. 1.11 and 1.12 we see that height is unchanged but range is diminished. Plots reflecting even stronger winds are shown in Fig. 1.13.

Code Listing 1.13: Relative velocity due to wind

```
#
ax=( -c1*(vx-vw))
ay=(g-c1*(vy   ))
#
```

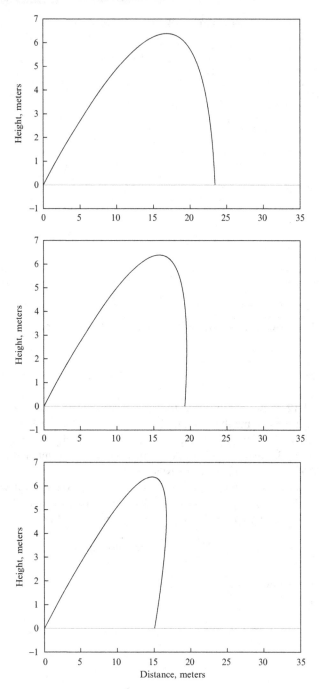

Fig. 1.13: Headwind trajectory plots. *Top* to *bottom*: 20 mph, 30 mph, and 40 mph

Fig. 1.14: Early users of modern computing systems. *Left*: A tank in Tunisia, 1943, the World War II campaign that motivated ENIAC. *Right*: Ada Lovelace, 1838 (Images courtesy of the U.S. Army and NASA. Tank photo credit U.S. Army Military History Institute, WWII Signal Corps Photograph Collection)

ENIAC, Z1, and ABC

The idea of a computer is not new. In the nineteenth century mechanical devices were built to perform otherwise difficult calculations. The first programmer was Ada Lovelace, shown in Fig. 1.14 alongside a World War II era tank, and U.S. Defense Department programming language Ada was named after her. During the North African Campaign our need to update artillery firing tables motivated ENIAC, shown in Figs. 1.15 and 1.16, the first programmable electronic computer.

Even though ENIAC is more famous now, the Z1 machine built in Germany was already programmable, and Iowa State University already had the electronic ABC.

While more elaborate equations are used in practice, each entry of a firing table based on our 2-D model would require finding the range x given the wind v_w and initial angle θ, assuming that v_0, g, and all other parameters are fixed. These ranges could be calculated in parallel and since each entry is independent of any other this is an "embarrassingly parallel" problem, so-called because the parallel code is relatively straightforward to write.

Besides having already generated such a firing table and simply looking up the answer, how could you find θ to hit a specific target range x_T given a known v_w?

Fig. 1.15: ENIAC, the Electronic Numerical Integrator and Computer. *Top*: Image courtesy of the U.S. Information Agency. *Bottom*: U.S. Army Photo

Fig. 1.16: ENIAC, continued. *Top*: U.S. Army Photo. *Bottom*: U.S. Army Photo

Fig. 1.17: Trajectory plot for free fall from a height of just under one mile with a tailwind of not quite 1 mph. Note carefully the vast difference between horizontal and vertical scales

Lab125: Free Fall

To simulate free fall we set $v_0 = 0.0$ and perhaps $y_0 = 1500.0$ meters, with a slight tailwind of $v_w = 0.447$ meters per second. Results are shown in Fig. 1.17 where we note the vast difference between horizontal and vertical scales.

When v_y stops changing the projectile has reached "terminal velocity" indicating that $a_y = 0$ because the two terms g and $c_1 v_y$, shown again in Code Listing 1.14 for reference, balance each other out. Detailed plots in Fig. 1.18 show the evolution of vertical velocity and acceleration over time.

Question: When would $a_x = 0$ and thus v_x stop changing, too?

Code Listing 1.14: Terminal velocity occurs when $a_y = 0$

```
#
ay=(g-c1*vy)
#
```

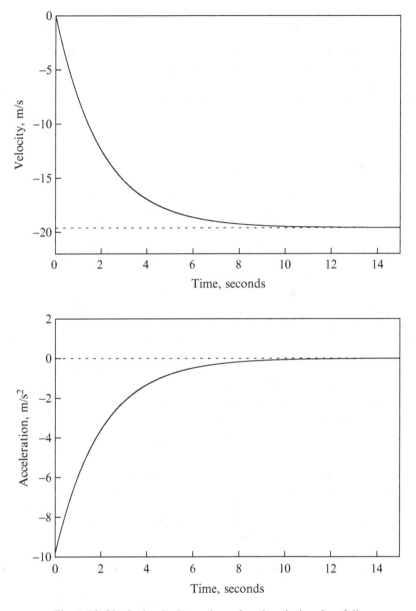

Fig. 1.18: Vertical velocity and acceleration during free fall

1.3 Lunar Module

Our final problem for this chapter involves landing on the Moon. Unlike the two previous problems our code will now have to allow the user to interact with a running program. Note that Fig. 1.19 contains an anachronism: the Earthrise background photo is from the Apollo 8 mission on 24 December 1968, but the *Eagle* lunar module photo is from Apollo 11 on 20 July 1969, the day before extravehicular activity.

Lab131: Uncontrolled Descent

We begin first with no user interaction because the animation alone requires your complete, focused attention. The underlying model is 1-D freefall with no air resistance as the lunar atmosphere is practically a vacuum. Code Listing 1.15 shows a complete program, written in Python 2 with Tk and PIL, and your assignment is to understand what it does.

Line 31 establishes that a_y is determined entirely by $g_M = -1.62 \, \text{m/s}^2$ and we note that compared to Earth's $g_E = -9.81 \, \text{m/s}^2$ the gravitational acceleration is only 16.5 % as strong on the Moon. So, when we conclude that our speed on impact is almost 40 mph keep in mind that this figure would be closer to 100 mph on Earth; well, only if air resistance is neglected... thank goodness for air! And parachutes!

Lines 14–16 are familiar, note however they are no longer contained in a loop but instead a function `tick` to control animation. Commands to make this animation work are underlined on Lines 11 and 24, and the call on Line 57 to the canvas object's `after` method starts the entire process with a request that "after 1 millisecond" the tick function should be called,

but it does not actually call the tick function itself.

The function is defined starting on Line 11 and takes no arguments. The conditional call on Line 24 keeps the process going (tick, tick, tick, tick, tick, ...) following the first call. In addition to facilitating animation we can also think of this repeated calling as taking the place of our main loop, with Line 23's `if`-statement acting like the "keep going" condition of a `while`-loop.

Of course only a single frame can be displayed on the screen at any one time and the graphics are repeatedly updated by Line 21 which moves our image of the *Eagle* as it falls. The illusion of crashing is maintained because Line 20 and Line 37 consider $y = 0$ to be only 70 % of the way downscreen, an ad hoc figure.

Curiously, the Tk system requires that the names `pmg1` and `pmg2` on Line 47 and Line 51 be different; otherwise, if the variable of a photo image is discarded then the corresponding Tk image will disappear (!) from the window.

Figure 1.20 shows our goal: landing on the moon instead of crashing.

Fig. 1.19: Descent of the lunar module (not shown to scale). *Top*: beginning free fall at an altitude of 100 meters, a contrived scenario. *Bottom*: crashing at over 40 mph (Images courtesy of NASA, lunar module photo credit Michael Collins)

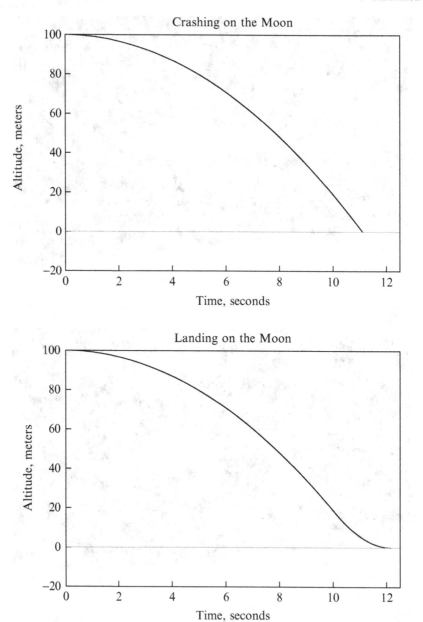

Fig. 1.20: Altitude over time during lunar descent. *Top*: crashing at over 40 mph. *Bottom*: controlled landing with vertical thrusters burning just before touchdown so that impact velocity is well under 2 mph

Code Listing 1.15: A complete program, written in Python 2 with Tk and PIL

```
1   ###############################################################################
2   #
3   # Chapter 1:    Simulation
4   # Problem 3:    Lunar Module
5   # Lab 1.3.1:    Uncontrolled Descent
6   #
7   ###############################################################################
8   from Tkinter import Tk,Canvas
9   from PIL      import Image,ImageTk
10  ###############################################################################
11  def tick():
12      global t,y,vy
13      #
14      t   += dt
15      y   += (vy*dt)
16      vy  += (ay*dt)
17      #
18      print t,y,vy
19      #
20      yp = 0.7*h/y0*(y0-y)
21      cnvs.coords(tkid,w/4.0,yp)
22      #
23      if y>0.0:
24          cnvs.after(1,tick)
25  #
26  ###############################################################################
27  w,h= 800,600
28  #
29  y0 = 100.0    # meters --> we must stipulate that images are not shown to scale
30  vy =   0.0    # m/s    --> so, assuming some previous arrangements at play here
31  ay =  -1.62   # m/s^2, acceleration due to gravity near the surface of the Moon
32  #
33  t  =    0.0
34  dt =    0.001
35  #
36  y  =    y0
37  yp =    0.7*h/y0*(y0-y) # linearly interpolate --> crash before the very bottom
38  #
39  print t,y,vy
40  ###############################################################################
41  #
42  root=Tk()
43  cnvs=Canvas(root,width=w,height=h,bg='black')
44  cnvs.pack()
45  #
46  img1=Image.open('earthrise.jpg').resize((w,h))
47  pmg1=ImageTk.PhotoImage(img1)
48  cnvs.create_image(w/2.0,h/2.0,image=pmg1)
49  #
50  img2=Image.open('eagle.jpg').resize((200,170))
51  pmg2=ImageTk.PhotoImage(img2)
52  tkid=cnvs.create_image(w/4.0,yp,image=pmg2)
53  #
54  f=('Times',14,'bold')
55  cnvs.create_text(w-110,h-15,text='Images courtesy of NASA.',font=f)
56  #
57  cnvs.after(1,tick)
58  root.mainloop()
59  #
60  # end of file
61  #
62  ###############################################################################
```

-15.59

Images courtesy of NASA.

Fig. 1.21: Controlled lunar descent where the *black rectangle* now artificially marks our landing site and the current velocity is indicated in meters per second (Images courtesy of NASA, lunar module photo credit Michael Collins)

Lab132: Controlled Descent

Now that our animation is working we can add user interaction. Code Listing 1.16 shows commands both to display current velocity v_y and also to fire vertical thrusters by pressing the spacebar. Figure 1.21 suggests further helping the user control for a soft landing by artificially marking the landing site.

Code Listing 1.16: Additional commands that allow for user interaction

```
def tick():
   cnvs.itemconfigure(tkid2,text='%0.2f'%vy)
#
def spacebar(evnt):
   global vy
   vy+=1.0   # another ad hoc figure
#
tkid2=cnvs.create_text(w-75,50,text='%0.2f'%vy,fill='white')
#
root.bind('<space>',spacebar)
```

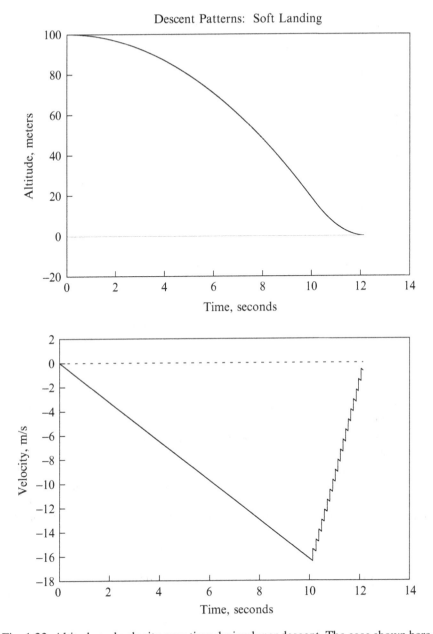

Fig. 1.22: Altitude and velocity over time during lunar descent. The case shown here is a "soft landing" where vertical thrusters are burned just after the 10 second mark

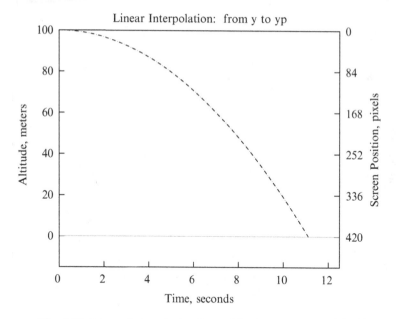

Fig. 1.23: Linear interpolation from altitude to screen position

Lab133: Descent Patterns

The "sawtooth curve" in Fig. 1.22's velocity plot reflected the fact that we instantaneously add 1.0 to v_y whenever the spacebar is pressed, because the code is easier to write this way, but in reality the act of burning thrusters would itself take time making the v_y curve smoother.

Translating from altitude to screen position, as shown again in Code Listing 1.17 for reference, assumes $\frac{yp-0}{0.7h-0} = \frac{y-y_0}{0.0-y_0}$ which calculates yp from a known y given that 0 (screen position) corresponds to y_0, and $0.7h$ with 0.0 (altitude). Vertical coordinates are often inverted as Fig. 1.23 shows because the upper-left corner tends to anchor a graphics window.

Your assignment is to generate the plots shown in Figs. 1.24, 1.25, and 1.26.

Code Listing 1.17: Linear interpolation of vertical position

```
#
yp=0.7*h/y0*(y0-y)
#
```

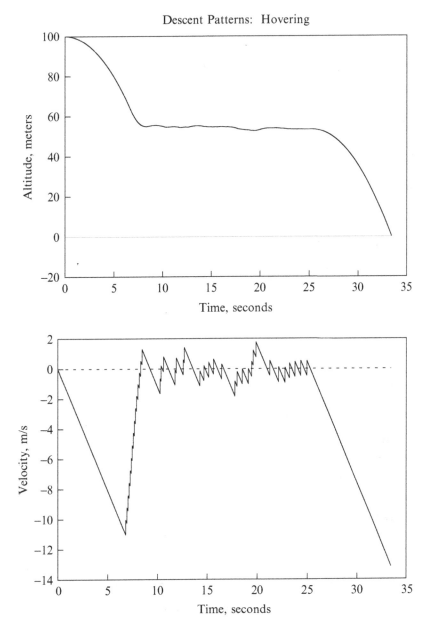

Fig. 1.24: Altitude and velocity over time during lunar descent. In this case the lunar module "hovers" mid-descent before crash landing at just under 30 mph

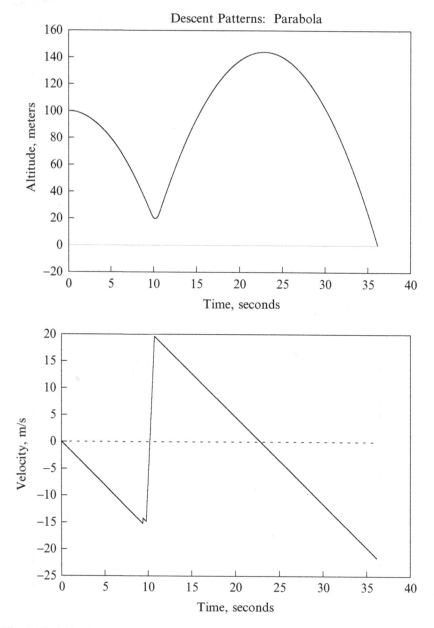

Fig. 1.25: Altitude and velocity over time during lunar descent. In this case the lunar module performs a secondary "climb" before crash landing at just under 50 mph

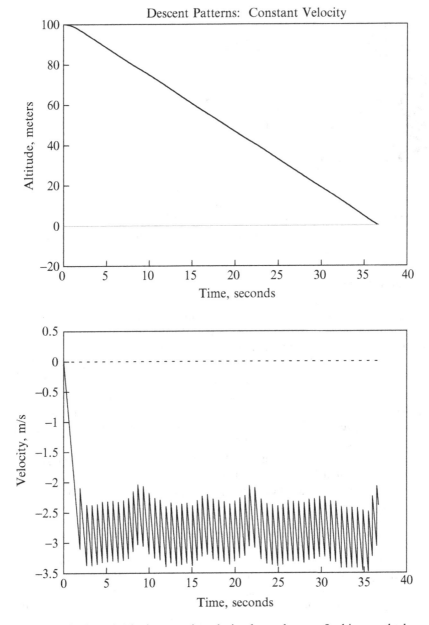

Fig. 1.26: Altitude and velocity over time during lunar descent. In this case the lunar module maintains a constant velocity "profile" and lands safely at just over 5 mph

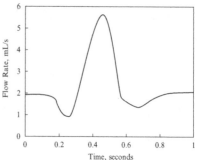

Fig. 1.27: Computing applied to diagnosis and treatment. *Left*: An operating room during surgery, the culmination of extensive preparation. *Right*: Typical volumetric bloodflow profile from a single heartbeat, one starting point toward the expansion of knowledge (Image courtesy of the U.S. Army, photo credit C. Todd Lopez)

Medical Applications

Simulation has become sufficiently robust to influence medicine by, for instance, modeling the flow of blood within our bodies. Figure 1.27 suggests one piece of minimal information needed for diagnosis or treatment.

The process by which arteries transport blood away from our heart is similar to incompressible flow in a pipe where viscosity dictates the interaction with tissue lining the inner wall of our blood vessels. Unlike a lunar module descent velocity, bloodflow is periodic and the waveform pattern is repeated with each heartbeat.

These flows were studied by Poiseuille in the nineteenth century while the more general set of equations were, around the same time, formulated by both Navier and Stokes. An inviscid model had already been developed by Euler in the eighteenth century using Newton's famous second law of motion from the seventeenth century. But only in the latter twentieth century have computers become powerful enough to apply these models to practical cases.

So, science waited centuries for machines to catch up. Now what?

Running an experiment that may pose some danger to a human patient is governed chiefly by issues related to medical ethics, and we choose to err on the side of "first, do no harm." Again this makes simulation an attractive technique but also when a patient's life-and-death (!) depends on proper diagnosis and treatment then the accurate performance of our code takes on a fundamentally different level of importance.

Fig. 1.28: Controlled lunar descent with limited fuel availability. Remaining fuel is indicated by the number of times vertical thrusters may be burned, initially 20 (Images courtesy of NASA, lunar module photo credit Michael Collins)

Lab134: Limited Fuel

While we can press the spacebar as often as we like in real life the lunar module contained a limited amount of fuel. Code Listing 1.18 shows one way to model limited fuel in our code and Fig. 1.28 shows the current fuel level communicated to the user; when the number reaches 0 then we can no longer fire the thrusters.

Code Listing 1.18: Limited fuel where we track the current level remaining

```python
def spacebar(evnt):
    global vy,u
    #
    if u>0:
        #
        vy+=1.0
        u -=1
```

Fig. 1.29: As shown, vertical thrusters fire at regular intervals but we do not even use all our fuel. Upon modification of the firing schedule your author's best effort was a $v_y = -0.17$ m/s landing, under 0.5 mph

Lab135: Optimal Strategy

Do you think the target rectangle, fuel indicator, and velocity text are easy to use? An alternative would be to define a strategy in the code and thus automate the entire process (i.e., no longer use the spacebar at all). Code Listing 1.19 specifies a firing schedule based on current elapsed time with results, crash, reported in Fig. 1.29.

Code Listing 1.19: Control of vertical thrusters with a firing schedule

```
def tick():
    global t,y,vy,i
    #
    if i<len(fs) and t>=fs[i]:
        vy+=1.0
        i +=1
    #
#
i=0
fs=[ 1.0, 2.0, 3.0, 4.0, 5.0, 6.0, 7.0, 8.0, 9.0,10.0,\
     11.0,12.0,13.0,14.0,15.0,16.0,17.0,18.0,19.0,20.0]
```

Chapter 2
Graphics

Curiosity might ask *how* an image is built at all. In this chapter we consider three different representations: a bitmap assigning colors to each pixel, a scalable model requiring later calculations to render the image, and an even higher level specification where the underlying details are completely hidden from view.

As an example of our first distinction, PPM stands for "portable pixel map" and this format specifies literally hundreds of thousands of red-green-blue color values in very large image files. SVG is "scalable vector graphics" where images contain only a geometric description of lines and curves, thus reducing file size by delaying the pixel-by-pixel rendering process. This approach has the advantage that enlarging a vector image is immune from any pixelation issues the corresponding bitmap would face, but it also means the original image must be conceived in terms of geometric objects which is not trivial for, say, a photograph.

Figure 2.1 shows three example image files, the last of which is a photograph. Code Listing 2.1 shows a simple way to produce the first example.

Fig. 2.1: Example image files: gold, silver, and Olympus Mons, Mars, the largest known volcano (Image courtesy of NASA from the Viking 1 mission, 22 June 1978)

Code Listing 2.1: A complete program, written in Python 2 with PIL

```
from PIL import Image
img=Image.new('RGB',(100,75),(212,175,55)) # gold
img.save('gold.png') # formats: JPG, PPM/PGM, EPS
```

© Springer International Publishing 2016

S. Torbert, *Applied Computer Science*, DOI 10.1007/978-3-319-30866-1_2

Table 2.1: A pixel map for a very small 5 × 5 image

	[0]	[1]	[2]	[3]	[4]
[0]	·	·	·	·	·
[1]	·	·	·	·	·
[2]	·	·	·	·	·
[3]	·	·	·	·	·
[4]	·	·	·	·	·

2.1 Pixel Mapping

Table 2.1 shows a very small 5 × 5 image. If one byte is used to specify each color value and there are 25 pixels, then we require only 75 bytes to store all RGB data for this entire image. (Each dot stores red 0-255, green 0-255, blue 0-255 at the pixel center.) PPM files also include a header listing such information as the width and height of our image, but the header does not scale with image size in the same manner that the amount of color data will.

Lab211: Circle π

Figure 2.2 shows one quadrant of the unit circle within a unit square. Your assignment is to produce such an image. Code Listing 2.2 specifies a side-length m which in turn determines the total number of pixels $n = m^2$. The variable count will be used to count-up how many of these n pixels are also inside our unit circle.

In addition, Fig. 2.3 shows pixelation when a smaller bitmap is enlarged, either by direct calculation or with interpolation of the color values. Free tools are available for this kind of image manipulation.

Code Listing 2.2: Initializing variables

```
#
m=600
n=m*m
#
count=0
#
```

Fig. 2.2: One quadrant of the unit circle within a unit square. Note y-coordinates are often inverted in graphical systems, for either interactive windows or stored files

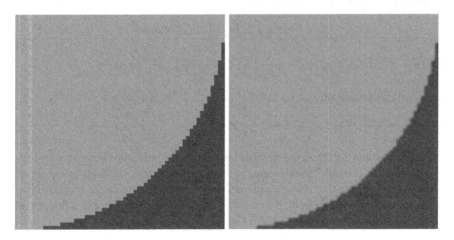

Fig. 2.3: Pixelation when a smaller bitmap is enlarged. *Left*: direct calculation. *Right*: linear interpolation of colors using the GNU Image Manipulation Program

Table 2.2: Image size, computed value of π, and associated runtime

Size m	Computed π	Runtime, seconds
100	3.1428	0.05
1000	3.141676	1.32
10,000	3.14159388	132.31

Table 2.3: Size (no image), computed value of π, and associated runtime

Size m	Computed π	Runtime, seconds
100	3.1428	0.01
1000	3.141676	0.88
10,000	3.14159388	88.53
1,000,000	3.141592655988	11.55*

The area of a circle is $A = \pi r^2$ and so for the unit circle, where $r = 1$, area is $A = \pi$. For only one quadrant area is $A = \pi/4$. If the n pixels in our image represent a unit square with area $A = 1$, the number of pixels inside the circle will relate to n by a $\pi : 4$ ratio. Since we count these pixels in our code we may approximate π with improving accuracy as n increases, shown in Tables 2.2 and 2.3 with runtimes for an Intel® Core i7-940 chip.

Code Listing 2.3 converts from pixel coordinates to unit coordinates, and also shows how the putpixel method is called on an image to set the RGB color value of a single pixel. Of course the value of (x, y) rather than (xp, yp) determines if a point is inside the unit circle or not.

Code Listing 2.3: Initializing variables

```
#
x=(xp+0.5)/m # plus one-half --> pixel center!
#
img.putpixel((xp,yp),(160,32,240)) # purple
#
```

Figures 2.4 and 2.5 detail the runtime improvements possible whenever a critical observation can be made. In this case, our observation is that we might avoid some of the individual counting if we can pre-determine that an entire range of pixels falls inside (or outside) of the circle. By counting all those pixels together in a line, or in a box, fewer checks are required and a significant speed-up occurs.

---

* Estimated runtime for size $m = 10^6$ is over ten days. Our eleven second runtime is based on a more efficient calculation suggested on the next page. A common story: the necessity of running a large problem is what compels us to consider a more sophisticated technique in the first place.

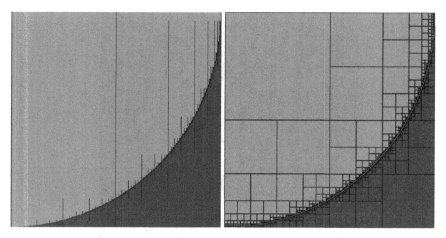

Fig. 2.4: Circle divide-and-conquer. *Left*: binary search, only the marked pixels are checked and all other pixels are classified automatically. *Right*: quadtree, a similar idea in 2-D where only the corners of each box are checked. In general our goal is to localize calculations for larger sizes along the edge of the circle, where they matter

Fig. 2.5: Divide-and-conquer savings. For the previous size $m = 10^6$ result we might alternatively process the $10^6 \times 10^6 = 1$ trillion pixels in parallel using over 75,000 computers to achieve the same runtime performance, thus we tend to prefer a better algorithm to a bigger computer (or more computers) when possible

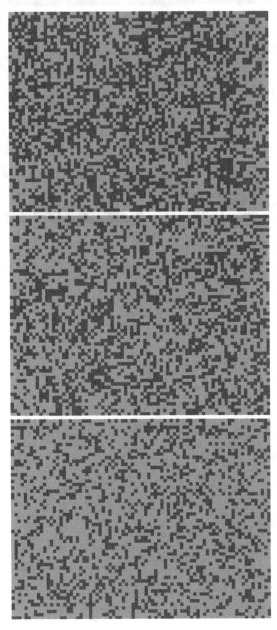

Fig. 2.6: Percolate pixelate. *Top* to *bottom*: $p = 0.5$, $p = 0.6$, and $p = 0.7$

Lab212: Percolate Pixelate

Consider an 80×60 image where each pixel is colored green with probability p and purple with probability $1 - p$. Algorithm 2.1.1 enlarges this image to 800×600 by converting each pixel into a 10×10 block of 100 pixels. Figure 2.6 shows typical results for $p = 0.5$, $p = 0.6$, and $p = 0.7$. Later in Chap. 5 we will ask:

For what probabilities will there be a green pathway connecting all four sides?

If each pixel has at most four neighbors (i.e., not counting diagonals) then it appears the $p = 0.5$ image does not have a path while $p = 0.7$ clearly does. For $p = 0.6$ it is not at all obvious what will happen in general.

This question is related to "percolation" or the flow of fluids (e.g., groundwater) in porous material such as rock or a layer of sediment (or the flow of boiling water through coffee grounds in a percolator). Percolation theory applies graph algorithms and statistics to what was originally conceived as a physical science problem.

Also, in this context pixelation is actually helpful because it aids the human eye in tracing pathways across the image. It would not be desirable to use a "better" image with some form of interpolation, although eventually this will not matter once we have coded an automatic tool to determine if such a pathway exists.

Another example of a helpful pixelation is shown in Figs. 2.7 and 2.8.

Algorithm 2.1.1 Enlarging a smaller bitmap image

1: **while** $y = 0 \to 59$ **do**
2:    **while** $x = 0 \to 79$ **do**
3:       **if** $random < p$ **then**
4:          $color = green$
5:       **else**
6:          $color = purple$
7:       **end if**
8:       **while** $i = 0 \to 9$ **do**
9:          $ynew = 10y + i$
10:         **while** $j = 0 \to 9$ **do**
11:            $xnew = 10x + j$
12:            $pixel(xnew, ynew) = color$
13:         **end while**
14:       **end while**
15:    **end while**
16: **end while**

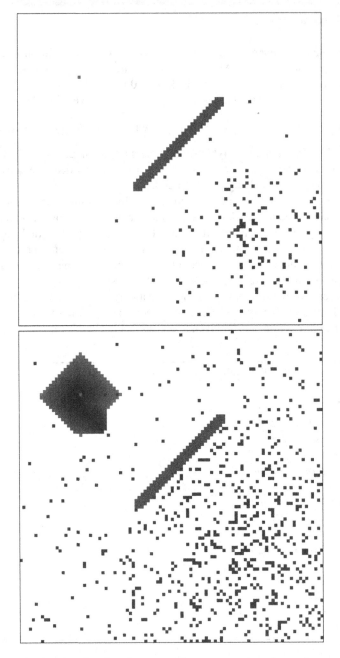

Fig. 2.7: A simple visualization for a complex system. Ants leave the nest (*bottom right quadrant*) moving randomly. An obstacle (*middle*) blocks their path to a food source (*top left quadrant*). As they return food to the nest, ants release a pheromone that both diffuses and evaporates. *Top*: after 75 steps. *Bottom*: after 375 steps

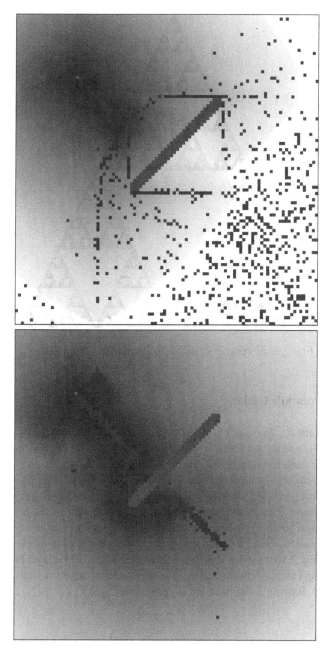

Fig. 2.8: A simple visualization for a complex system, continued. Blocks of 6×6 pixels show ants, obstacle, or pheromone concentration. Where pheromone has not yet spread the ants continue to move randomly. Based upon *Ant Foraging Revisited* by Liviu Panait and Sean Luke. *Top*: after 450 steps. *Bottom*: after 750 steps

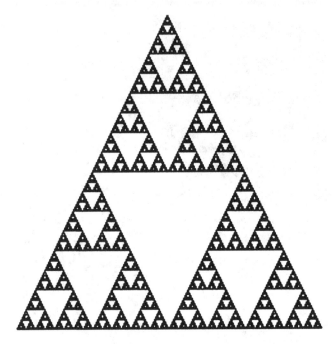

Fig. 2.9: Sierpinski's Gasket, formed by a Chaos Game

Lab213: Sierpinski's Gasket

Fix three points P_1, P_2, and P_3. As shown in Fig. 2.9 these are $P_1 = (0.5, 0.1)$, $P_2 = (0.1, 0.9)$, and $P_3 = (0.9, 0.9)$, if we map the image pixel coordinates to unit square coordinates. Randomly initialize a fourth point $P = (x, y)$, pick one of the three fixed-points also at random, then move P halfway toward that point and draw the corresponding pixel in your image. Now repeat: randomly pick one of the three fixed-points, move P halfway from its current position, and draw the pixel.

Our result is a famous fractal called Sierpinski's Gasket and this random drawing process is known as a Chaos Game. Experiment with the total number of loops for yourself but Fig. 2.10 provides some guidance for a 300×300 image. Note how we reach "carrying capacity" because there are only so many pixels to draw.

Alternative drawing techniques are suggested in Fig. 2.11.

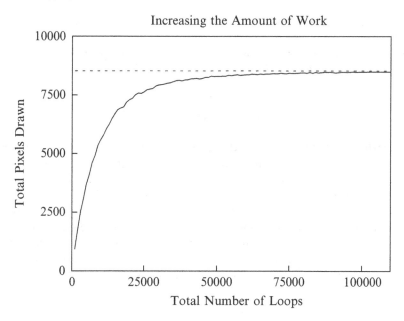

Fig. 2.10: Diminishing marginal returns. Since there are only so many pixels to draw eventually more-and-more looping introduces fewer-and-fewer new pixels

Fig. 2.11: Pascal's Triangle. Obviously we could generate a similar image geometrically by starting with a whole triangle and recursively discarding the middle quarter. Or, here we suggest a technique based on coloring the even-odd values in Pascal's much used triangle, albeit for a sample this small our image is quite pixelated

Lab214: Draw a Line

A line may be drawn from a point $P_1 = (x_1, y_1)$ to another point $P_2 = (x_2, y_2)$ by looping from $t = 0.0$ to $t = 1.0$ and drawing pixels corresponding to:

$$x = x_1 + t \cdot (x_2 - x_1)$$
$$y = y_1 + t \cdot (y_2 - y_1)$$

Clearly when $t = 0.0$ we draw P_1, when $t = 1.0$ we draw P_2, and for $0.0 < t < 1.0$ the pixels in-between are drawn. However, if we choose dt too large then we may draw a "dotted" line and for dt too small we waste time re-drawing the same pixels over and over again.

As shown in Fig. 2.12 your assignment is to draw 50 random lines where P_1 is chosen inside a circle with radius $r = 75$ (all units are in pixels and the image size is 250×250) and P_2 is outside that circle but inside another concentric circle with $r = 125$. Note the lack of anti-aliasing here, as in Jack Bresenham's famous line drawing algorithm but later addressed by Xiaolin Wu.

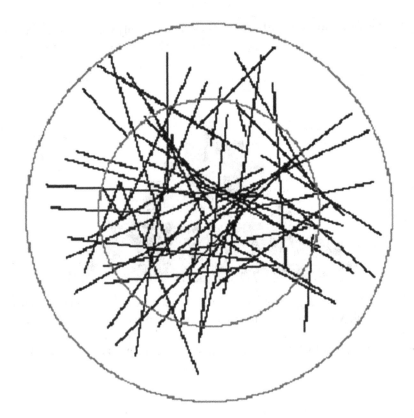

Fig. 2.12: Random lines in concentric circles

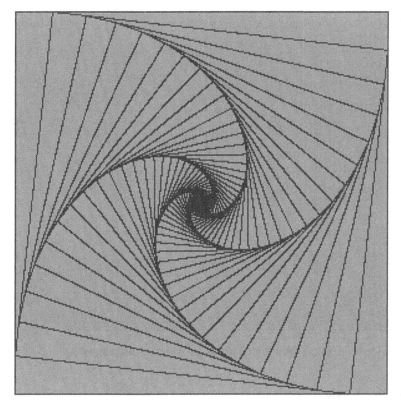

Fig. 2.13: Chasing turtles draw the "envelope" of four spirals

Lab215: Chasing Turtles

We might imagine the spirals shown in Fig. 2.13 are the result of four bugs chasing each other, or four dogs, or even penguins. But as the next problem will use turtles we imagine them initialized at the corners of a box and looking only at their nearest clockwise neighbors. Steps "simultaneously" move the turtles 10% of the way toward these nearest neighbors while also drawing the lines of sight. Code Listing 2.4 shows RGB color codes for tan and dark green.

Code Listing 2.4: Color codes for tan and dark green

```
img=Image.new('RGB',(w,h),(210,180,140)) # tan
#
img.putpixel((x,y),(0,100,0)) # dark green
```

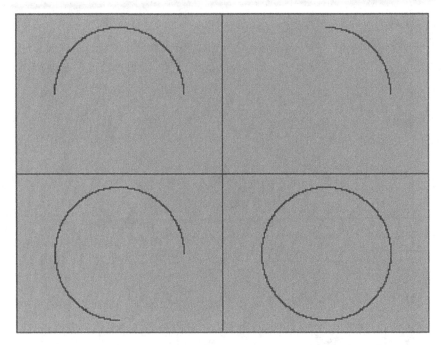

Fig. 2.14: Four quadrants of a circle being drawn

Drawing a Circle

Figure 2.14 shows the four quadrants of a circle being drawn.

Code Listing 2.5 shows the code for all four quadrants only. In the first quadrant the angle stops at $\pi/2$, in the second quadrant at π, and in the third at $3\pi/2$.

In all cases the radius is constant while the angle changes. If instead we were drawing a line then the radius would change while the angle remained constant.

Code Listing 2.5: All four quadrants of a circle being drawn

```
#
t=0.0
while t<2.0*pi:
    x=int(xc+r*cos(t)+0.5)
    y=int(yc-r*sin(t)+0.5) # invert the y-coordinate
    #
    img.putpixel((x,y),(0,100,0))
    #
    t+=0.001
```

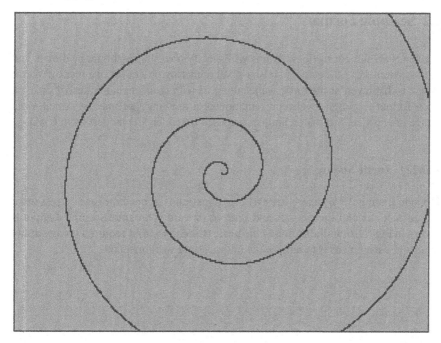

Fig. 2.15: Four revolutions of a spiral being drawn

Drawing a Spiral

Figure 2.15 shows four revolutions of a spiral being drawn, and Code Listing 2.6 shows how to check if a pixel (x, y) is out-of-bounds in an image.

In a spiral, both the radius and angle change together at the same time.

Code Listing 2.6: Four revolutions of a spiral being drawn

```
#
t=0.0
while t<8.0*pi:
    #
    r=???
    #
    ...
    #
    if 0<=x<w and 0<=y<h: img.putpixel((x,y),(0,100,0))
    #
    t+=0.001
```

2.2 Scalable Format

Like an SVG file our turtle programs will specify how shapes should be drawn, and both systems delay the actual pixel-by-pixel rendering process until either the vector image is displayed or the turtle walks along its path (carrying a marker, of course). Each format is a high-level representation of a drawing that may be scaled to an image of any size. Similar techniques are used to render 3-D models from CAD.

Lab221: Turtle Square

In Code Listing 2.7 a general drawline function is defined on Line 11, essential turtle functions on Lines 25–45, and Line 46 onward is program specific. Output is shown in Fig. 2.16. Initialization of the turtle (Lines 54–56) is required for any drawing. Your assignment is to replace the ellipses with working code.

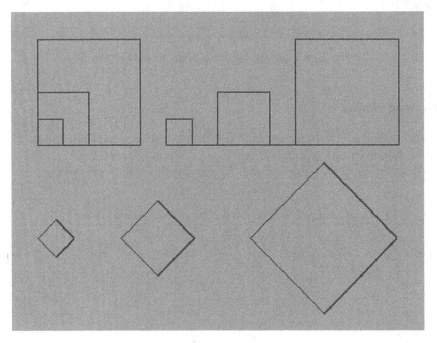

Fig. 2.16: Turtle square, rendered in a variety of sizes, sequences, and directions

Code Listing 2.7: An incomplete program is known as a "shell"

```
1    #############################################################################
2    #
3    # Chapter 2:    Graphics
4    # Problem 2:    Scalable Format
5    # Lab 2.2.1:    Turtle Square
6    #
7    #############################################################################
8    from PIL import Image
9    from math import cos,sin,pi
10   #############################################################################
11   def drawline(x1,y1,x2,y2):
12       #
13       t=0.0
14       while t<=1.0:
15           #
16           ...
17           #
18           x=int(x+0.5)                    # round to the nearest pixel
19           y=int(y+0.5)
20           img.putpixel((x,y), ... )
21           #
22           t+=0.001
23       #
24   #
25   def jump(xnew,ynew):
26       global xt,yt
27       #
28       xt=xnew
29       yt=ynew
30   #
31   def move(r):
32       global xt,yt
33       #
34       oldx,oldy=xt,yt
35       #
36       xt +=  r*cos(ht*pi/180.0)
37       yt += -r*sin(ht*pi/180.0)        # inverted
38       #
39       drawline(oldx,oldy,xt,yt)
40   #
41   def turn(dh):
42       global ht
43       #
44       ht+=dh                            # counterclockwise
45   #
46   def square(size):
47       #
48       ...
49       #
50   #
51   #############################################################################
52   img=Image.new('RGB',(320,240), ... )
53   #
54   xt =  20.0 # x-position of turtle
55   yt = 100.0 # y-position
56   ht =   0.0 # heading, in degrees
57   #
58   square(20.0)
59   ...
60   #
61   # end of file
62   #
63   #############################################################################
```

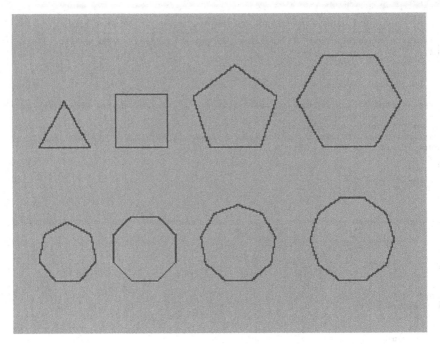

Fig. 2.17: Turtle poly, rendered for an increasing number of sides

Lab222: Turtle Poly

Figure 2.17 shows polygons with $n = 3, 4, 5, 6$ sides and side-length 40 pixels (top) and $n = 7, 8, 9, 10$ of side-length 20 pixels (bottom). Code Listing 2.8 shows how easy `square` is to write once the `poly` function is working.

Code Listing 2.8: A more general function

```
#
def poly(size,n):
    #
    ...
#
def square(size):
    #
    poly(size,4)
#
```

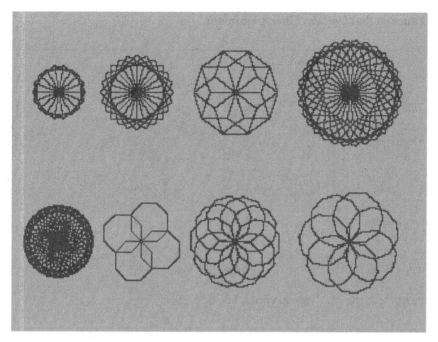

Fig. 2.18: Spin poly, rendered for a variety of patterns

Lab223: Spin Poly ´

Figure 2.18 shows polygons spinning in beautiful ways. The idea of turtles drawing vector graphics is not new and versions for many different programming languages might be used in a variety of contexts and education levels.

Our code uses "local" variables in drawline because values of t, x, and y are unimportant once the function has finished executing. But we use "global" variables in jump and turn because the values of xt, yt, and ht are essential in tracking our turtle as it moves across the image over time.

Function move uses each kind of "scope" and note how Python treats arguments like r, dh, and $size$ as copies* of the original. Local copies. By default an assignment in a function will create a local variable as with t and x and y. When you see the global command it is telling Python not do this, that the variable is not local, as with a turtle's data xt and yt and ht.

---

* Variables stored with a "pointer" and passed to a function may be altered but not by assignment.

A Function that Updates Global Variables

```
#
def jump(xnew,ynew):
    global xt,yt
    #
    xt=xnew
    yt=ynew
    #
#
...
#
xt= 20.0
yt=100.0
#
jump(0.0,0.0)
#
print xt,yt      # output is 0.0 0.0
#
```

A Function that Creates Local Variables Instead

```
#
def jump(xnew,ynew):
    #
    xt=xnew
    yt=ynew
    #
#
...
#
xt= 20.0
yt=100.0
#
jump(0.0,0.0)
#
print xt,yt      # output is 20.0 100.0
#
```

Lab224: Spin Spiral

Figure 2.19 shows polygons spinning while side-length also changes. In particular, the circular spiral was inspired by an automated lawn mower project where the gap width between layers had to match the specific width of the real-life lawn mower. Can you draw this spiral with a *purposeful* gap width?

Turtle code may be organized into modules as Python does with its Tk library, math module, the Python Imaging Library (PIL), and even a built-in turtle:

http://docs.python.org/library/turtle.html

A drawline function might be in a general-use module for graphics separate from the turtle library. (In fact PythonWare® put ImageDraw in PIL.) Programs could access these resources with the same kind of import statements we have been using for "official" modules. We did not organize our programs this way only because the code is small and, especially when beginning, ease-of-use is highly valued.

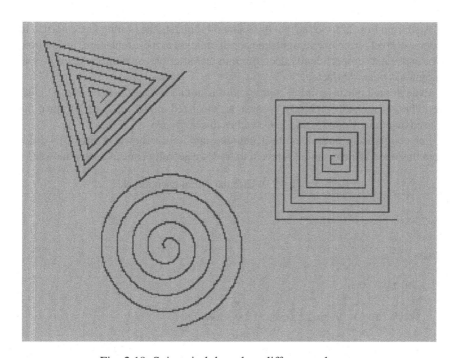

Fig. 2.19: Spin spiral, based on different polygons

Circular Spiral

Since the "polygon" is a circle do not change the "side-length" but rather the radius.

Imagine that the automated lawn mower is tethered; a stake is placed at the center of the spiral then a rope is tied to both the stake and the lawn mower.

If the knot in the rope is loose and turns freely around the stake then the lawn mower will trace out a circle. However, if the knot is fixed and the rope wraps around the stake as it turns then the lawn mower will trace out a spiral.

As more rope is wrapped the lawn mower moves closer to the stake. Figure 2.20 shows how each revolution must wrap an amount of rope equal to the desired gap. But this decrease happens gradually with each forward movement, not all at once.

Say the "side-length" is 1.0 and assume this is sufficiently small to approximate a circular arc. What angle θ is traced out by a circular arc 1.0 unit in length?

For a radius r the entire circumference is $2\pi r$ and one revolution is $360°$, or 2π radians. So:

$$\frac{\theta}{2\pi} = \frac{1.0}{2\pi r} \quad \Rightarrow \quad \theta = 1.0/r$$

Also from Fig. 2.20 we see that this same θ is equal to the turning angle needed to "course correct" from our straight-line approximation to the circular arc. In addition, we can use it to proportionally decrease r so that after one revolution the entire gap amount has been subtracted.

Even though our inspiration is physical it is not necessary for our code to model the tethering scenario precisely because an idealized model may still produce the desired outcome. Code Listing 2.9 sketches this approach.

For comparison, how does the technique previously shown in Fig. 2.15 differ from this one? Which is more relevant to how we actually control a lawn mower?

Code Listing 2.9: Circular spiral pseudocode

```
#
r=???
#
gap=???
#
while r>0.0:
    #
    move(1.0) # sufficiently small
    #
    # calculate the turning angle ...in radians
    #
    turn(...)
    #
    # decrease r proportional to the gap amount
    #
```

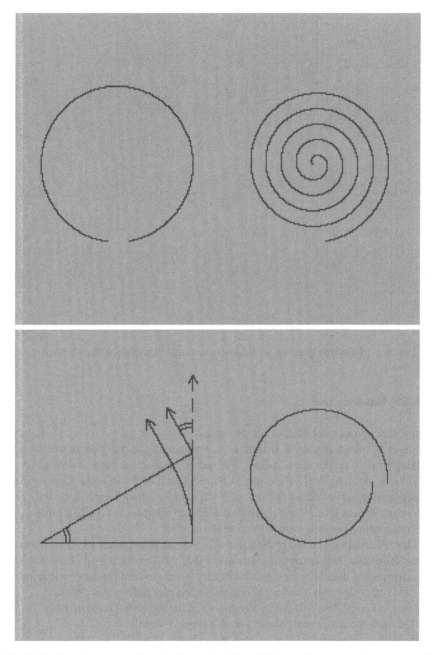

. Fig. 2.20: Development of a circular spiral. *Top*: If the radius is not changed at all then a circle is drawn instead of a spiral. *Bottom*: A straight-line approximation, shown larger here, closely resembles a circular arc on a sufficiently small scale; also, the change in radius after one revolution must equal the desired gap amount

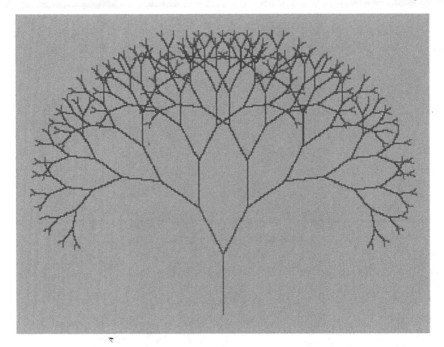

Fig. 2.21: Random tree, we might also use random angles at each branching

Lab225: Random Tree

Figure 2.21 shows most, but not all, of a tree.

The tree was drawn by 800 turtles, each beginning at the bottom-middle and walking straight up the trunk, making 799 redundant lines on the first step alone.

Then, at random, half of the turtles branched left and half right. This random branching process continued for nine total steps (eight left-right decisions) with size decreasing at each level. Some turtles walked the exact same total path as others had, not contributing anything new to the overall drawing.

This redundancy is more probable at all levels as time passes so we again have diminishing marginal returns, as shown in Fig. 2.22. Depending on how much the size changes the details of these plots will vary but the overall characteristic remains the same: there are only so many pixels and eventually each one is drawn.

Later in Chap. 5 we will see an alternative technique called *recursion* that can be used to draw the entire tree precisely with a single (!) turtle.

Other recursive possibilities are shown in Figs. 2.23 and 2.24.

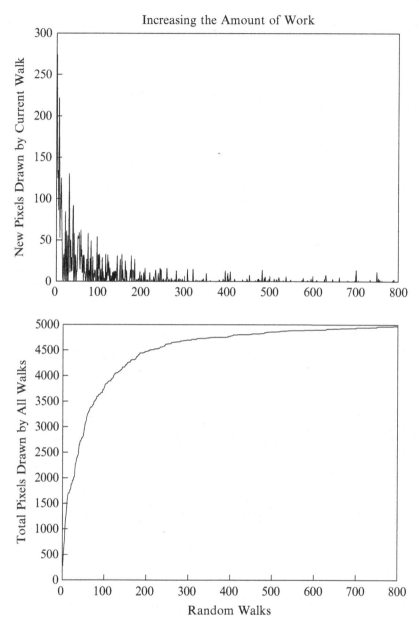

Fig. 2.22: Diminishing marginal returns. *Top*: new pixels drawn by current walk.
Bottom: total pixels drawn by all walks, shown after each new walk

Fig. 2.23: Turtle recursion fractal gallery. *Top*: Snowflake curve. *Bottom*: Dragon

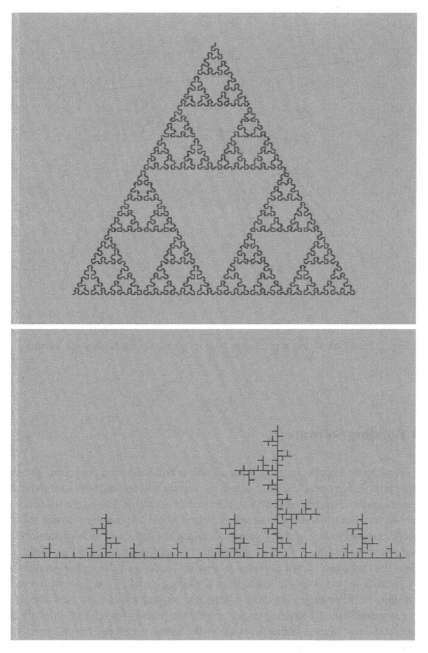

Fig. 2.24: Turtle recursion fractal gallery, continued. *Top*: Sierpinski's Gasket, again, yet another drawing technique. *Bottom*: Lines "growing" out of other lines

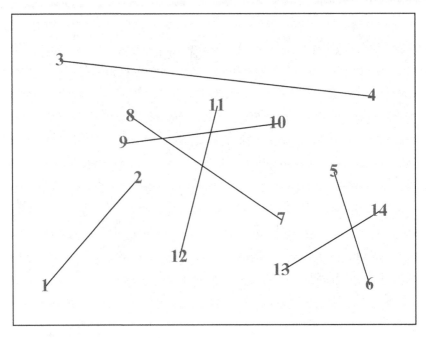

Fig. 2.25: Click count, where your own program need not show the counts

2.3 Building Software

We return to interactive graphics with a goal to build drawing programs for non-commercial sketchwork. The final suggested version will include both tool and color selectors and is a starting point for a full piece of software. The user experience is foremost so we continually ask ourselves: "How would someone new to this react?" Feature-creep must be carefully guarded against as clutter and incoherence do not make a positive interface. Keep in mind what the application is supposed to be.

Writing "software" is not the same as writing "code" because code is written for only yourself to run. Software has to keep working even after you leave the room so we need to make assumptions about what a typical user would want, and also what they can actually do. Comparing vector graphics to pixel-by-pixel data, software is a representation at an even higher level where the user does not see *any* of the details. In the same way, as a coder you are like the user when importing a library you did not write, or a library that you wrote but just not recently.

Lab231: Click Count

Our first idea is to respond when the user clicks the mouse; every second click we draw a line connecting the two previous click locations. The click count numbers shown in Fig. 2.25 have been added only to show how the lines were drawn and they should not be present in your own version unless you really mean for them to be a part of someone's sketch.

Code Listing 2.10 is a shell where the event-object evnt knows the (x, y) location of each mouse click. Note again how we must specify that *count*, x, and y are defined at the global scope since function click contains an assignment statement for each of these variables. In this manner their values will persist between successive calls (i.e., between successive clicks). Line 30 assumes we want left-clicks rather than right-clicks, thus Button-1 rather than Button-3.

Code Listing 2.10: A shell of a program

```
 1 ###############################################################################
 2 #
 3 # Chapter 2:   Graphics
 4 # Problem 3:   Building Software
 5 # Lab 2.3.1:   Click Count
 6 #
 7 ###############################################################################
 8 from Tkinter import Tk,Canvas
 9 ###############################################################################
10 #
11 w,h=400,300
12 #
13 count = ...
14 #
15 def click(evnt):
16     global count,x,y
17     #
18     count += ...
19     #
20     if ...
21         x=evnt.x
22         y=evnt.y
23     else:
24         cnvs.create_line(x,y,evnt.x,evnt.y,fill='black')
25 #
26 root=Tk()
27 cnvs=Canvas(root,width=w,height=h,bg='#FFFFF0') # ivory
28 cnvs.pack()
29 #
30 root.bind('<Button-1>',click)
31 root.mainloop()
32 #
33 # end of file
34 #
35 ###############################################################################
```

Fig. 2.26: Polyline, right-click ends each chain, left-click starts the next one

Lab232: Polyline

Figure 2.26 shows a "polyline" where a right-click ends each chain. Key events are also shown in Code Listing 2.11 and function exit is from the sys module.

Code Listing 2.11: Mouse click events and quitting the program

```
#
def click(evnt):
    ...
#
def rightclick(evnt):
    ...
#
def quit(evnt):
    exit(0)
#
root.bind('<Button-1>',click)
root.bind('<Button-3>',rightclick)
root.bind('q',quit)
#
```

Lab233: Pencil Draw

Of course when we draw a pencil sketch we do not press the paper only at the
endpoints of a line but at every single point. We can implement this feature using
drag events as shown in Code Listing 2.12 and Fig. 2.27, a quick "review" session.

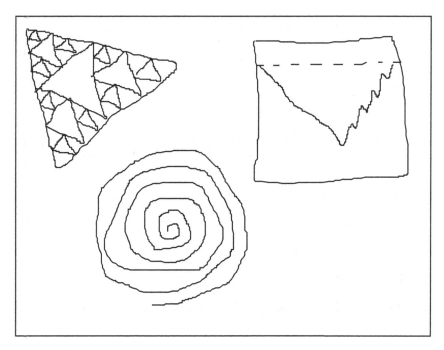

Fig. 2.27: A stroll down memory lane with highlights from our previous labs

Code Listing 2.12: Mouse dragged event

```
#
def click(evnt):
    ...
#
def drag(evnt):
    ...
#
root.bind('<Button-1>',click)
root.bind('<B1-Motion>',drag)
#
```

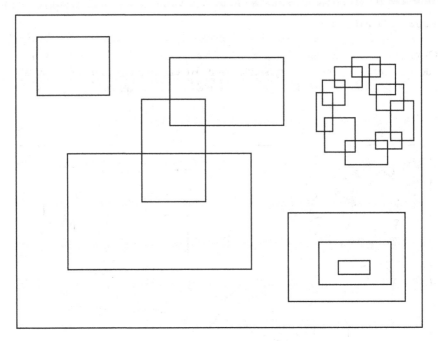

Fig. 2.28: Rectangles, updated as you drag, fixed only when the button is released

Lab234: Rectangles

Figure 2.28 shows rectangles where each is drawn dynamically using commands shown in Code Listings 2.13 and 2.14, so you see it grow as the mouse is dragged.

Code Listing 2.13: Rectangle commands

```
#
tkid=cnvs.create_rectangle( ... ,fill='')
cnvs.coords(tkid, ... )
#
```

Code Listing 2.14: Mouse released event

```
#
def release(evnt):
    ...
#
root.bind('<ButtonRelease-1>',release)
#
```

Fig. 2.29: Motion and more motion, toward a WYSIWYG system

Motion and Double-Click

We might also like to see the growing line update as we move (not drag) in our previous line and polyline programs, before a click sets the second or next endpoint. The `coords` command works the same on lines as it does on rectangles, shown in Fig. 2.29 where a line is growing first from Point 5 to Point 6 and then, presumably, a future Point 7. Code Listing 2.15 shows how to respond to mouse motion events when no button is being pressed.

In addition, Code Listing 2.16 shows a double-click event we might use to connect the last endpoint of a polyline back to the first endpoint. In this case we must assume the location of our first click was remembered at the time it happened because it cannot be reconstructed later.

Code Listing 2.15: Mouse motion event

```
#
def move(evnt):
    . . .
#
root.bind('<Motion>',move)
#
```

Code Listing 2.16: Double-click event

```
#
def doubleclick(evnt):
    . . .
#
root.bind('<Double-Button-1>',doubleclick)
#
```

Lab235: Graffiti Tool

Figure 2.30 shows all our previous drawing tools as options, plus a color selector, and one last new feature: spray paint. (Disclaimer, vandalism is a crime.) This tool presents a number of coding challenges most notably that the spray paint should still work when the button is pressed even if the mouse is not moving, so drag events alone are not sufficient.

One solution is to use animation where a click sets some Boolean variable true, the subsequent release sets it false, and drag events update the (x, y) location. All the while our `tick` function is drawing random 1×1 rectangles somewhere in a circle centered at the current (x, y) and so long as the mouse button is still being pressed. In this context random points clustered near the center of a circle actually match the reality of a spray can.

The graffiti icon displayed among the tools will be different with each run of the program unless we set an explicit random number seed. (In the same way exact replication of simulation results may be obtained, an important requirement of any experiment.) You might also consider including a fill-the-area tool, a cut-and-paste option, and some facility for saving the current picture to an image file.

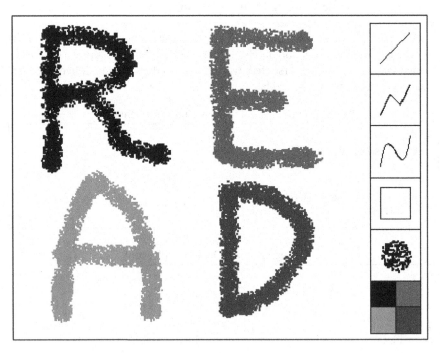

Fig. 2.30: Graffiti tool, one of many options our users enjoy

Chapter 3
Visualization

An ability to create graphics in various forms is not the same as an ability to say something important *and understandable* using graphics. A famous high-quality example is shown in Fig. 3.1 by Charles Jospeh Minard, from 1861. This map depicts a shrinking French army in 1812, first invading Russia and then retreating.

Fig. 3.1: Napoleon's 1812 invasion of Russia, by Charles Joseph Minard, 1861

Illuminating complex data is not easy. In particular, when conclusions influence a political decision we must guard against what Orwell observed: "The great enemy of clear language is insincerity." The same holds for graphics where a picture's worth a thousand words either sincerely spoken or not. Of course Minard did not use a computer in the nineteenth century but our focus will be on images that are either impossible to produce without a computer or at least very much easier with one.

© Springer International Publishing 2016
S. Torbert, *Applied Computer Science*, DOI 10.1007/978-3-319-30866-1_3

Fig. 3.2: Cholera outbreak in London, by John Snow, 1854. The *black dots* represent cholera deaths and stacks of these can be found near the Broad Street water pump

3.1 Geospatial Population Data

Figure 3.2 is from John Snow's 1854 study of a cholera outbreak. The concentration of cases near a particular water source, made obvious by Snow's drawing, led to an understanding that contaminated water was involved in spreading the disease.

The composite image of our nighttime Earth shown in Fig. 3.3 was produced by NASA from satellite data. Such a picture is not only impossible but probably also unimaginable without advanced technology, and a time-traveler from the past could not be expected to make much sense of it. However, it should say a lot to us.

County-level results from Florida's contentious *Bush v. Gore* presidential election are shown in Fig. 3.4. Geospatial plots have become much easier to build since polygon shape files for U.S. regions, as well as election results, are now publicly accessible on the Internet:

https://www.census.gov/geo/maps-data
http://results.elections.myflorida.com

Article 2, Section 1 of the U.S. Constitution says the Electoral College is based on states, not counties, but since administration of elections happens at the county level (local level) this is where complaints were made.

Fig. 3.3: Earth at night, a high-tech composite of satellite data, 27 November 2000 (Image courtesy of NASA, production credit C. Mayhew and R. Simmon)

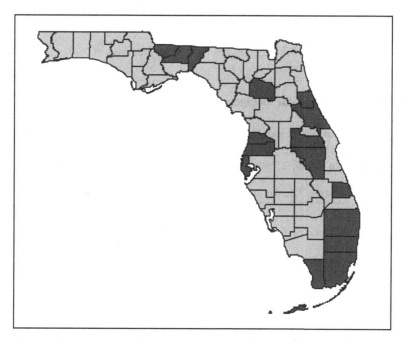

Fig. 3.4: Florida county-level presidential election results from 7 November 2000 (Counties are light gray if won by George W. Bush and dark gray if won by Al Gore)

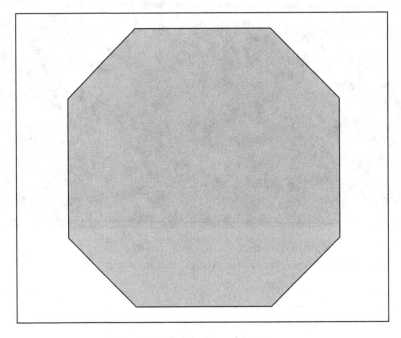

Fig. 3.5: Slightly irregular octagon

Lab311: Slightly Irregular Octagon

A missing piece in our Florida graphic is population data because a landslide win in one county could equate with many close wins in others. We begin by drawing a polygon as shown in Fig. 3.5 where our octagon is almost regular but not quite.

Code Listing 3.1: An example polygon specified by hand in a list

```
#
xy=[(2,1),(1,2),(-1,2),(-2,1),(-2,-1), ... ]
xyp=[]
#
j=0
while j<len(xy):
    x,y=xy[j]
    ...
    xyp.append((xp,yp)) # scale 5-95% of screen height
    j+=1
#
cnvs.create_polygon(xyp,fill='#CCC',outline='black')
#
```

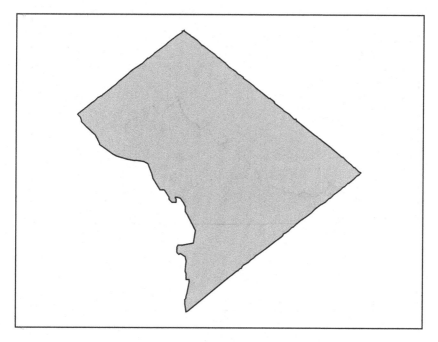

Fig. 3.6: Washington, D.C

Lab312: Washington, D.C.

We do not "find" the min/max in Code Listing 3.1 since they are plainly -2 and 2. However, the 49 regions of the contiguous U.S. require $O\left(10^5\right)$ vertices and those, in turn, require a data file. Code Listing 3.2 reads the vertices used by Fig. 3.6.

Code Listing 3.2: Polygon data from a file being read into a list

```
#
data=open('lab312.txt','r').read().split()
xy=[]
#
j=0
while j<len(data):
    x=float(data[j])
    j+=1
    y=float(data[j])
    j+=1
    ...
    xy.append((x,y))
#
```

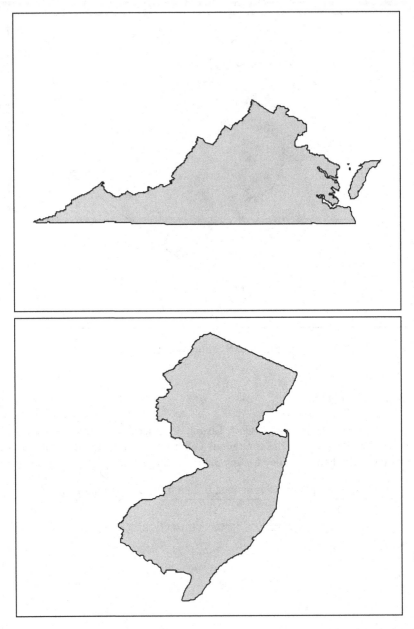

Fig. 3.7: Aspect ratio. *Top*: Virginia, four polygons, 2.88 : 1, wider than it is tall.
Bottom: New Jersey, represented by a single polygon, 1 : 1.46, taller than it is wide

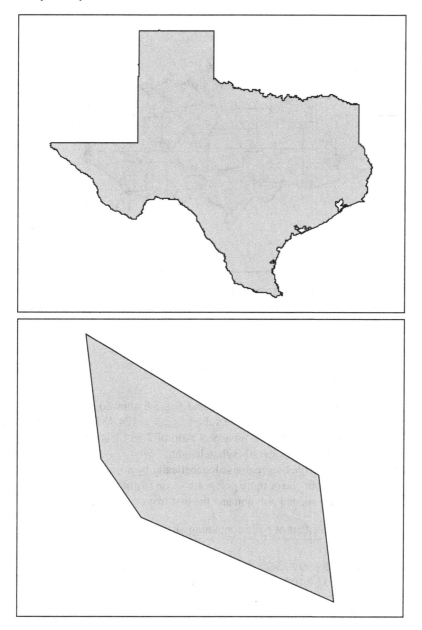

Fig. 3.8: Vertices. *Top*: One of the two polygons for Texas has over 6000 vertices. *Bottom*: Pea Patch Island, in Delaware, depicted as a pentagon. Not shown to scale

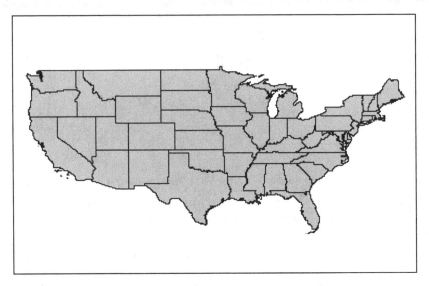

Fig. 3.9: Contiguous U.S. regions: 48 states and Washington, D.C

Lab313: Contiguous United States

Figure 3.7 showed aspect ratio examples and Fig. 3.8 showed two vastly different polygons. Figure 3.9 shows extreme values $x_{min} = -124.733$, $x_{max} = -66.950$,
$y_{min} = 24.545$, and $y_{max} = 49.384$, an aspect ratio of 2.33 : 1 not 1.33 : 1 (or 4 : 3)
and we are now bound by width rather than height.

Our cleaned-up data file lists regions alphabetically by postal abbreviation where
each region may contain one or more polygons. Code Listing 3.3 shows the last two
vertices of Alabama's second polygon and the first two of Arkansas's only polygon.

Code Listing 3.3: Part of a file containing all 49 contiguous U.S. regions

```
...
-88.1665689999999955    30.2492550000000016
-88.1884692736000062    30.2469340542000005
END_ONE_POLY
END_ALL_POLY
AR
-94.4760497582000056    36.4993199124999990
-94.4568835367000048    36.4993666550000029
...
```

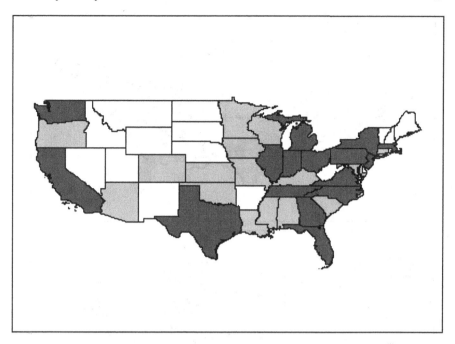

Fig. 3.10: Population data from Census 2000

Lab314: Population Data

Figure 3.10 distinguishes regions with more than 5,600,000 people, those with fewer than 2,675,000, or in-between. Code Listing 3.4 reads the population data and stores it in a hashtable by associating keys with values: print htable['DC']

Code Listing 3.4: Population data from a file being read into a hashtable

```
#
data=open('lab314.txt','r').read().split()
htable={}
#
j=0
while j<len(data):
    key=data[j]
    j+=1
    val=int(data[j])
    j+=1
    #
    htable[key]=val
#
```

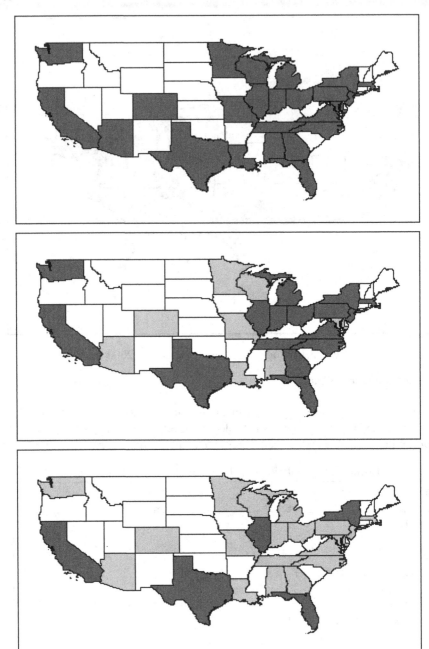

Fig. 3.11: Population data from Census 2000, continued

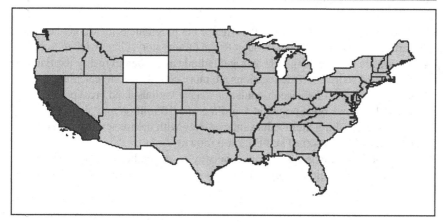

Fig. 3.12: Population data from Census 2000, continued

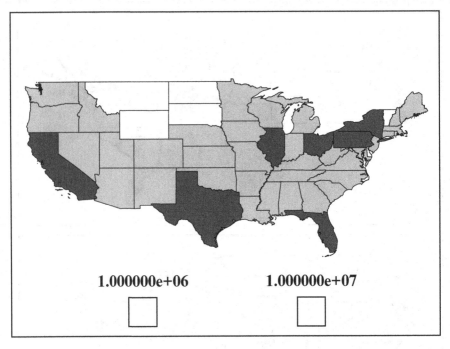

Fig. 3.13: Dynamic updates, a breakpoint is modified if the mouse hovers over its corresponding square as the scroll-wheel turns… and the colors change immediately!

Lab315: Dynamic Updates

Latitude is measured north-south of the equator but longitude is measured east-west of the (arbitrary) prime meridian through Royal Observatory, Greenwich in London, England. We are treating longitude as x and latitude as y when in reality the Earth is almost spherical so true surface locations are more complicated to calculate.

Figures 3.11 and 3.12 showed population data at various fixed breakpoints.

Figure 3.13 shows breakpoints at 1 million and 10 million and also suggests a technique for controlling these values interactively with mouse scroll-wheel events, implemented as Button-4 (up) and Button-5 (down).

Line 48 of Code Listing 3.5 shows one way to remember the Tk ID numbers associated with each region's polygons. This is important because as the breakpoints change we may need to re-color:

```
cnvs.itemconfigure(tkidnum,fill=color)
```

This command is run inside two loops: one loop for all the regions and then another for all the polygons of each region, where only the color values are changing.

These same techniques could instead be used to zoom as in Figs. 3.14, 3.15, 3.16, and 3.17.

Code Listing 3.5: A shell for part of a program

```
1  ##############################################################################
2  #
3  # Chapter 3:   Visualization
4  # Problem 1:   Geospatial Popluation Data
5  # Lab 3.1.5:   Dynamic Updates
6  #
7  # https://www.census.gov/geo/maps-data/data/cbf/cbf_state.html
8  # http://pe.usps.com/text/pub28/28apb.htm
9  #
10 ##############################################################################
11 ...
12 data=open('lab313.txt','r').read().split()
13 tkid={}
14 name=None
15 #
16 j=0
17 while data[j]!='END_FILE':
18     #
19     if name==None:
20         name=data[j]
21         tkid[name]=[]                    # current region has yet to add a Tk ID#
22         xy=[]
23     #
24     elif data[j]=='END_ONE_POLY':
25         #
26         # current polygon now has all its (x,y) vertices
27         #
28         xyp=[]
29         #
30         j=0
31         while j<len(xy):                # loop over the polygon's (x,y) vertices
32             x,y=xy[j]
33             ...
34             xyp.append((xp,yp))
35             j+=1
36         #
37         # fill color is based on population data
38         #
39         if ...
40             color='#646464'             # dark gray
41         elif ...
42             color='#C0C0C0'             # light gray
43         else:
44             color='#FFFFFF'             # white
45         #
46         tkidnum=cnvs.create_polygon(xyp,fill=color,outline='black')
47         #
48         tkid[name].append(tkidnum)  # add this Tk ID# to current region's list
49         #
50         xy=[]
51     #
52     elif data[j]=='END_ALL_POLY':
53         name=None
54     #
55     else:
56         ...
57         xy.append((x,y))                # add one point to this polygon's xy-list
58     #
59     j+=1
60 #
61 ...
62 #
63 # end of file
64 #
65 ##############################################################################
```

Fig. 3.14: Zoom. *Top*: The path of the Mississippi River forms an "exclave" of Kentucky, highlighted in the upper-right quadrant, near where Missouri also shares a border with Arkansas and Tennessee. *Bottom:* Lake Michigan, water now in gray

Fig. 3.15: Zoom, continued. Top: San Francisco Bay. Bottom: Long Island Sound. By changing the range of values (x_{min}, x_{max}) and (y_{min}, y_{max}), either directly in the code or interactively during the run, any feature may be examined in greater detail

Fig. 3.16: Features. *Top*: Pacific Northwest. *Bottom*: Gulf of Mexico

Fig. 3.17: Features, continued. *Top*: Plymouth Rock. *Bottom*: Jamestown

3.2 Particle Diffusion

Consider again a random walk but now in 2-D rather than 1-D and with hundreds of particles not just one, bringing us closer to our previous atmospheric example.

Lab321: Mean Free Path

The motion of particles in a petri dish may be modeled by choosing, repeatedly, a random angle for each particle's direction and then moving a distance equal to the so-called "mean free path," representing an expected length of travel between successive collisions that would alter a particle's direction. Thus, by picking a new random angle after each movement our result will approximate what would have happened if we had modeled the actual collisions.

```
cnvs.move(tkid[j],dx,dy)
```

In our code we go a step further and assume the existence of a lattice constraining all particle motion to one of only four nearest neighbors: up, down, left, or right.

1000

Fig. 3.18: Diffusion after 1000 steps where all particles began at the center

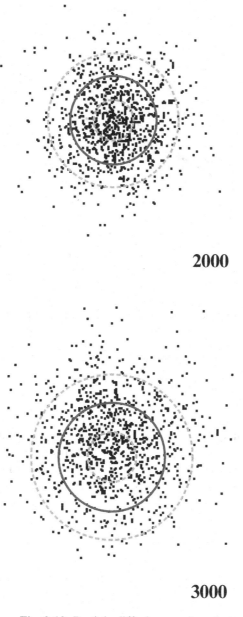

2000

3000

Fig. 3.19: Particle diffusion, continued

Fig. 3.20: Average distance, measured from the particles' shared starting location

Lab322: Average Distance

If the center is at (xc, yc) and some particle P_i is at (x_i, y_i) then the straight-line distance d_i is such that $d_i^2 = (x_i - xc)^2 + (y_i - yc)^2$. Figures 3.18 and 3.19 showed the average distance growing over time and Fig. 3.20 shows the same information in a single graphic without also showing the particles. Another measurement called the "root mean square" is shown too, as well as the square root of elapsed time.

$$AVG = \frac{1}{N} \sum_{i=0}^{N-1} \sqrt{(d_i^2)}$$

$$RMS = \sqrt{\left(\frac{1}{N} \sum_{i=0}^{N-1} d_i^2 \right)}$$

In calculating RMS, the square root in d_i and the square in the formula cancel each other out; ignore both to avoid performing useless calculations.

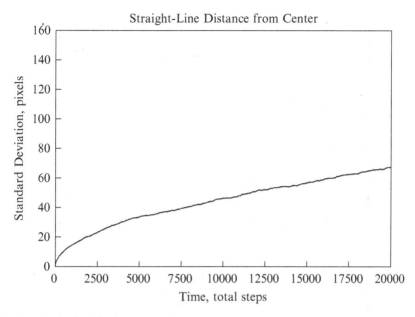

Fig. 3.21: Standard deviation, measuring the concentration of data near the average

Lab323: Standard Deviation

An increasing average distance tells us the particles are moving away from the center but it does not tell us they are moving away from each other; how do we know they are not all making the exact same movements together, or that a tight circle is not maintained with an expanding radius? Answer: calculate the standard deviation.

Figure 3.21 tells us the particles are spreading out away from each other. If we call the average distance μ then the standard deviation σ is calculated by:

$$\sigma = \sqrt{\left(\frac{1}{N} \sum_{i=0}^{N-1} (\mu - d_i)^2 \right)}$$

The two dashed circles in the previous plots were shown with a radius of one standard deviation above and below the average. Observation indicates that the area between these two circles accounts for almost 70% of our particles.

2500

Fig. 3.22: A second Tk window is used to animate a normal distribution probability curve as the particles are moving, shown here after 2500 steps

Code Listing 3.6: Adding a second Tk window to a single program

```
1  ##############################################################################
2  #
3  # Chapter 3:    Visualization
4  # Problem 2:    Particle Diffusion
5  # Lab 3.2.4:    Animate Normal Curve
6  #
7  ##############################################################################
8  from Tkinter import Tk,Canvas
9  from random   import random
10 from math     import sqrt,pi,exp
11 ##############################################################################
12 ...
13 #
14 # probability density function
15 #
16 def pdf(x,avg,sd):
17     if sd==0.0:          # special case... at time=1 all particles have d_i=1.0
18         if x==1.0:
19             return 1.0    # so... probability is 1.0 (certain) here
20         else:
21             return 0.0    # and... probability is 0.0 (impossible) elsewhere
22     else:
23         #
24         # general case...
25         #
26         return 1.0/(sd*sqrt(2.0*pi))*exp(-1.0*(x-avg)*(x-avg)/(2.0*sd*sd))
27 #
28 ##############################################################################
29 #
30 root=Tk()
31 cnvs=Canvas(root,width=w,height=h,bg='white')
32 cnvs.pack()
33 #
34 root2=Tk()
35 cnvs2=Canvas(root2,width=w,height=h,bg='white')
36 cnvs2.pack()
37 #
38 ...
39 root.mainloop()
40 #
41 # end of file
42 #
43 ##############################################################################
```

Lab324: Animate Normal Curve

As shown in Fig. 3.22 and Code Listing 3.6 we interpolate y from 0.0 to 0.03 and
assume a normal distribution with formula:

$$y = \frac{1}{\sigma\sqrt{2\pi}} \cdot e^{-(x-\mu)^2/(2\sigma^2)}$$

Note that x is measured in pixels for raw screen distance with no interpolation so
we scale only by a factor of 2, but since y is a probability it must be scaled by the
window height or our curve will appear exceedingly small.

Code Listing 3.7: Drawing a curve point-by-point, and a vertical line

```
#
def tick():
    ...
    #
    xp=0
    while xp<w:
        #
        # scale by a factor of 2
        #
        x=xp/2.0
        #
        # calculate the point on our curve
        #
        y=pdf(x,avg,sd)
        #
        # scale by the window height
        #
        yp=int(h-h*(y/0.03)+0.5)
        #
        # draw the point in pixel coordinates
        #
        cnvs2.coords(tkid2[xp],xp,yp,xp+1,yp+1)
        xp+=1
    #
    # vertical line at x=AVG
    #
    yavg=pdf(avg,avg,sd)
    yp=int(h-h*(yavg/0.03)+0.5)
    xp=int(2.0*avg+0.5)
    cnvs2.coords( ... ,xp,h-1,xp,yp)
    #
    ...
```

Lab325: Model Parameters

The vertical line in Fig. 3.23 is at $x = \mu$ and the horizontal line has length σ. Code Listing 3.7 shows how to draw our curve point-by-point and also how to draw the vertical line. What happens to the vertical and horizontal lines over time?

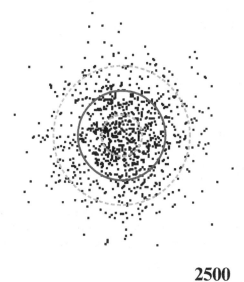

2500

Fig. 3.23: *Vertical* and *horizontal lines*, the model parameters

Code Listing 3.8: Bins form a histogram to check our model assumptions

```
#
def tick():
    ...
    #
    j=0
    while j<bins:
        #
        # current coordinates of this bin
        #
        x1,y1,x2,y2=cnvs2.coords( ... )
        #
        # desired height of this bin
        #
        y=bincount[j]/(1.0*num)/((w/2.0)/num_bins)
        #
        # translate bin height to pixel coordinates
        #
        y1=int(h-h*(y/0.03)+0.5)
        #
        # only the bin height changes !!!
        #
        cnvs2.coords( ... ,x1,y1,x2,y2)
        j+=1
    #
    ...
```

Animate Bins → Histogram

But the normal distribution assumption is wrong! Distance cannot be less than zero so an entire "tail" is cut off. Code Listing 3.8 and Fig. 3.24 show this by grouping the particles into various bins, forming a histogram.

As the bin width decreases (i.e., as the number of bins increases) an accurate model's curve would closely match the observed distribution of particles. You might use arrow keys to interactively change the bin settings...

```
root.bind('<Left>',leftarrow)
```

...but be careful, with only num=1000 particles too many bins will ruin any model.

Also, to avoid this truncation issue we could initialize the particles along a circle of radius 100, instead of clumped together, as shown in Figs. 3.25 and 3.26.

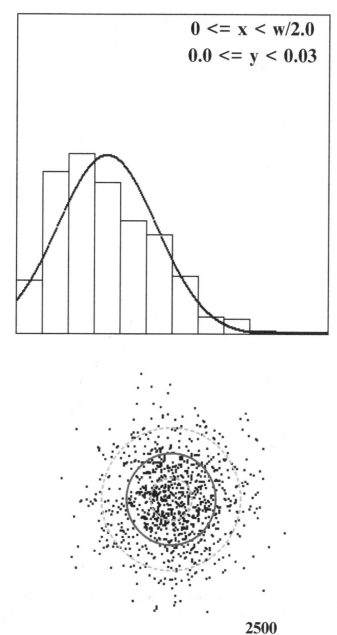

Fig. 3.24: A histogram for the observed particle distances indicating that our assumption of a normal distribution requires correction

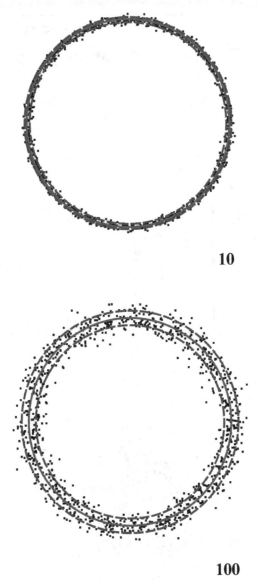

10

100

Fig. 3.25: No truncation. *Top*: Particles are initialized along a circle of radius 100.
Bottom: Drifting to the center, and zero-distance truncation, is a prolonged process

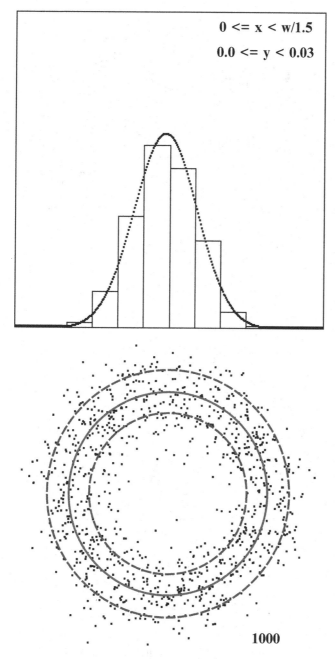

Fig. 3.26: No truncation, continued. *Top*: Bin *x*-values are changed to account for the increased distance of each particle. *Bottom*: Still drifting to zero-distance truncation

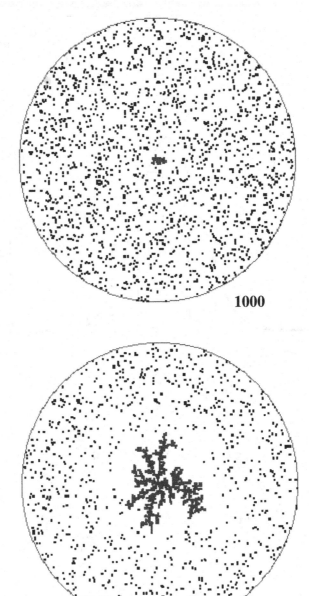

Fig. 3.27: Diffusion limited aggregation

Diffusion Limited Aggregation

A petri dish limits each particle's motion, shown in Figs. 3.27 and 3.28 with a uniform distribution at time zero. Fix one particle in place at the center. If a particle occupies an adjacent lattice point of any fixed-particle then it becomes fixed itself. In this way a crystalline-like "aggregation" develops as the number of fixed particles grows over time. These tendrils make it difficult for a still-traveling particle to reach the interior of the structure.

This is not an embarrassingly parallel problem because the location where one particle becomes fixed will influence where other particles can continue to move freely. Thus, this problem is said to be *coupled*. Two parallel options are possible.

First, if each parallel node tracks particles at any location then we must communicate where they become fixed. Each node might send a broadcast message to the entire group, or we could designate a "manager" node to collect everyone's information one-by-one and then make a single broadcast.

Alternatively, this application lends itself to *spatial decomposition*. If each node only tracks particles in a particular region of space, they only need to communicate fixed-particles on their boundary and only to that nearest-neighbor node. Of course if a particle leaves its region then a node will have to communicate this as well.

50000

Fig. 3.28: Diffusion limited aggregation, continued

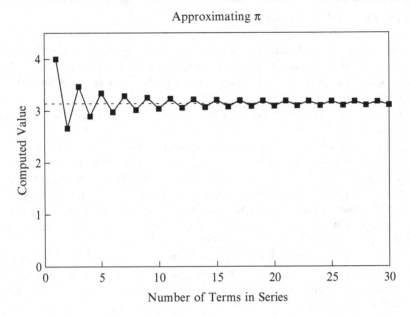

Fig. 3.29: Plot values, showing both alternating terms and convergence to π

3.3 Approximating π

Consider again how to calculate digits of π but now using series approximations such as Gregory's series, centuries-old (!) and based on $\tan 45° = \tan(\pi/4) = 1$.

$$\frac{\pi}{4} = \frac{1}{1} - \frac{1}{3} + \frac{1}{5} - \frac{1}{7} + \frac{1}{9} - \frac{1}{11} + \cdots$$

Lab331: Text Output

A cumbersome way to visualize this series is shown in Table 3.1 where we output the approximation as each new term is added. Note the *very* slow convergence.

Lab332: Plot Values

Since the sign alternates and the denominator grows we can bound our error without even knowing (!) the true value, as shown in Fig. 3.29 for the first 30 terms.

Table 3.1: Text output of a slowly converging series

Step	Computed π	Current term	Sign	Denom
1	4.0000000000000000	1.0000000000000000	1.0	1.0
2	2.6666666666666670	−0.3333333333333333	−1.0	3.0
3	3.4666666666666668	0.2000000000000000	1.0	5.0
4	2.8952380952380956	−0.1428571428571428	−1.0	7.0
5	3.3396825396825403	0.1111111111111111	1.0	9.0
6	2.9760461760461765	−0.0909090909090909	−1.0	11.0
7	3.2837384837384844	0.0769230769230769	1.0	13.0
8	3.0170718170718178	−0.0666666666666667	−1.0	15.0
9	3.2523659347188767	0.0588235294117647	1.0	17.0
10	3.0418396189294032	−0.0526315789473684	−1.0	19.0
11	3.2323158094055939	0.0476190476190476	1.0	21.0
12	3.0584027659273332	−0.0434782608695652	−1.0	23.0
13	3.2184027659273333	0.0400000000000000	1.0	25.0
14	3.0702546177791854	−0.0370370370370370	−1.0	27.0
15	3.2081856522619439	0.0344827586206897	1.0	29.0
16	3.0791533941974278	−0.0322580645161290	−1.0	31.0
17	3.2003655154095489	0.0303030303030303	1.0	33.0
18	3.0860798011238346	−0.0285714285714286	−1.0	35.0
19	3.1941879092319425	0.0270270270270270	1.0	37.0
20	3.0916238066678399	−0.0256410256410256	−1.0	39.0
2001	3.1420924036835256	0.0002499375156211	1.0	4001.0
2002	3.1410931531214472	−0.0002498126405196	−1.0	4003.0
2003	3.1420919046819966	0.0002496878901373	1.0	4005.0
2004	3.1410936516248467	−0.0002495632642875	−1.0	4007.0
2005	3.1420914066759815	0.0002494387627837	1.0	4009.0
2006	3.1410941491342212	−0.0002493143854400	−1.0	4011.0
2007	3.1420909096625045	0.0002491901320708	1.0	4013.0
2008	3.1410946456525419	−0.0002490660024907	−1:0	4015.0
2009	3.1420904136386012	0.0002489419965148	1.0	4017.0
2010	3.1410951411827663	−0.0002488181139587	−1.0	4019.0
2011	3.1420899186013189	0.0002486943546381	1.0	4021.0
2012	3.1410956357278415	−0.0002485707183694	−1.0	4023.0
2013	3.1420894245477173	0.0002484472049689	1.0	4025.0
2014	3.1410961292907023	−0.0002483238142538	−1.0	4027.0
2015	3.1420889314748672	0.0002482005460412	1.0	4029.0
2016	3.1410966218742717	−0.0002480774001488	−1.0	4031.0
2017	3.1420884393798509	0.0002479543763947	1.0	4033.0
2018	3.1410971134814618	−0.0002478314745973	−1.0	4035.0
2019	3.1420879482597623	0.0002477086945752	1.0	4037.0
2020	3.1410976041151719	−0.0002475860361476	−1.0	4039.0

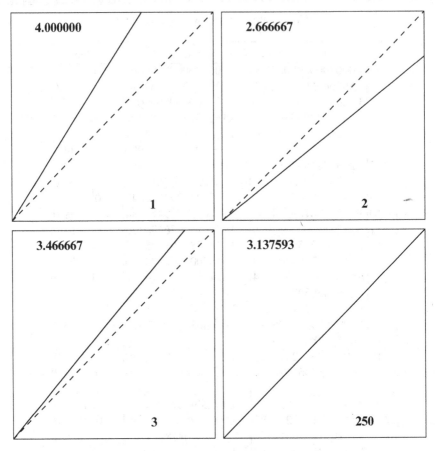

Fig. 3.30: Plot angle, dashed is $\pi/4$ and solid is our approximation

Lab333: Plot Angle

Since $\pi/4$ radians is a $45°$ angle we might plot our own approximation as an angle to compare. Figure 3.30 shows the first three steps and the 250th, which is so close that the angles cannot be distinguished. These drawings require `sin` or `cos` functions, defined either using the famous CORDIC algorithm or their own series:

$$\sin(x) = x - \frac{x^3}{3!} + \frac{x^5}{5!} - \frac{x^7}{7!} + \frac{x^9}{9!} - \frac{x^{11}}{11!} + \cdots$$

$$\cos(x) = 1 - \frac{x^2}{2!} + \frac{x^4}{4!} - \frac{x^6}{6!} + \frac{x^8}{8!} - \frac{x^{10}}{10!} + \cdots$$

Lab334: Another Series

An example of a non-alternating series for π is:

$$\frac{\pi^2}{6} = \frac{1}{1^2} + \frac{1}{2^2} + \frac{1}{3^2} + \frac{1}{4^2} + \frac{1}{5^2} + \frac{1}{6^2} + \cdots$$

Text output is shown in Table 3.2 where sign no longer matters (angles would approach $45°$ from only one side) but we must remember to square the denominator and take a square root after multiplying through by six. Runtime for 25 million terms was almost 14 seconds and the last term added is nearly zero in 16-digit floating-point representation, assuming use of the 64-bit IEEE standard format.

Table 3.2: Text output for the first 25 million terms

Step	Computed π	Current term	Denom=step^2
1	2.4494897427831779	1.0000000000000000	1.0
2	2.7386127875258306	0.2500000000000000	4.0
3	2.8577380332470415	0.1111111111111111	9.0
4	2.9226129861250305	0.0625000000000000	16.0
5	2.9633877010385707	0.0400000000000000	25.0
6	2.9913764947484185	0.0277777777777778	36.0
7	3.0117739478462142	0.0204081632653061	49.0
8	3.0272978566578428	0.0156250000000000	64.0
9	3.0395075895610533	0.0123456790123457	81.0
10	3.0493616359820699	0.0100000000000000	100.0
11	3.0574815067075627	0.0082644628099174	121.0
12	3.0642878178339279	0.0069444444444444	144.0
13	3.0700753718932203	0.0059171597633136	169.0
14	3.0750569155713614	0.0051020408163265	196.0
2500000	3.1415922716180411	0.0000000000001600	6.250000e+12
5000000	3.1415924626038212	0.0000000000000400	2.500000e+13
7500000	3.1415925262654896	0.0000000000000178	5.625000e+13
10000000	3.1415925580959025	0.0000000000000100	1.000000e+14
12500000	3.1415925771942814	0.0000000000000064	1.562500e+14
15000000	3.1415925899245529	0.0000000000000044	2.250000e+14
17500000	3.1415925990227356	0.0000000000000033	3.062500e+14
20000000	3.1415926058416219	0.0000000000000025	4.000000e+14
22500000	3.1415926111389916	0.0000000000000020	5.062500e+14
25000000	3.1415926153845746	0.0000000000000016	6.250000e+14

Table 3.3: Computer number systems

Decimal	Hexadecimal	Binary		Decimal	Hexadecimal	Binary
0	0	0000		8	8	1000
1	1	0001		9	9	1001
2	2	0010		10	A	1010
3	3	0011		11	B	1011
4	4	0100		12	C	1100
5	5	0101		13	D	1101
6	6	0110		14	E	1110
7	7	0111		15	F	1111

Floating-Point Representation

Computers do arithmetic in binary (base 2) because it is easier to build the machines that way. Table 3.3 counts in binary and also hexadecimal (base 16), a convenient intermediary because each hex digit translates directly to four binary digits (bits).

In the IEEE double-precision format a floating-point value stores 64-bits: one bit for the sign, 11 bits for the exponent, and 52 bits for the fraction. The exponent bits are assumed to be the actual exponent plus 1023 so that negative numbers, and two's complement integer conversion, are not required. However, there are special cases when the exponent bits are all the same. In the case of all ones we get either not-a-number (NaN) or an infinity. If the fractional bits are all zero then we have either positive or negative infinity, based on the sign. Otherwise it is NaN, meaning there are $2^{53} - 2 = O\left(10^{16}\right)$ different representations for not-a-number.

Generally our value is $\pm 1.F \times 2^{(E-1023)}$ where the 1 in front of the fraction need not be stored. If E is all zeros the value is $\pm 0.F \times 2^{-1022}$ instead. Thus, the smallest positive value is $2^{-1074} = O\left(10^{-324}\right)$, but arithmetic involving 1.0 and values less than machine epsilon $\varepsilon_{mach} = 10^{-16}$ has no effect, as we will soon see.

One by-product of this system is that many terminating decimals in base 10 are repeating "decimals" in base 2, perhaps most notably:

$$\frac{1}{10} = \frac{1}{15} + \frac{1}{30} = \frac{1}{15} + \frac{1}{2} \cdot \frac{1}{15} = 0.0\overline{0010}_2 + 0.0\overline{00001}_2 = 0.0\overline{0011}_2$$

Since these fractions are approximated in binary we must take great care in our code any time we want to compare two floating-point values exactly.

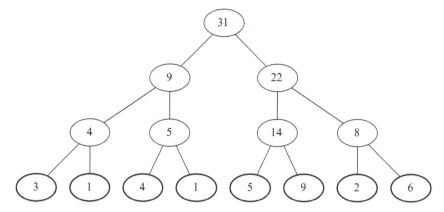

Fig. 3.31: Fine-grain parallelism, simultaneous summation in pairs

Fine-Grain Parallelism

Figure 3.31 suggests a technique for calculating any sum in parallel, in this case:

$$3+1+4+1+5+9+2+6 = 31$$

In serial we might initialize a variable `sum=0` and do a loop that adds each term:

`sum=3, sum=4, sum=8, sum=9, sum=14, sum=23, sum=25, sum=31`

However, as we have seen for series requiring a large number of terms, this loop may need to run for a long time. An alternative is to pair the terms up so that each pair-sum can be calculated simultaneously. Here `3+1=4` and `4+1=5` and `5+9=14` and `2+6=8` could all be calculated *at the same time* in parallel. This idea is repeatedly applied on the intermediate sums, so `4+5=9` and `14+8=22` at the next level, after which `9+22=31` gives the final result.

Rather than requiring $N = 25$ million loops we now need only $\log_2 N$ levels of this parallel tree. Since

$$\log_2 (25{,}000{,}000) < 25$$

we might speed up our run by a factor of a million! (In theory.) This is not an embarrassingly parallel problem or even one where spatial decomposition applies, but is known instead as *fine-grain* parallelism.

Additional examples are shown in Figs. 3.32, 3.33, 3.34, and 3.35.

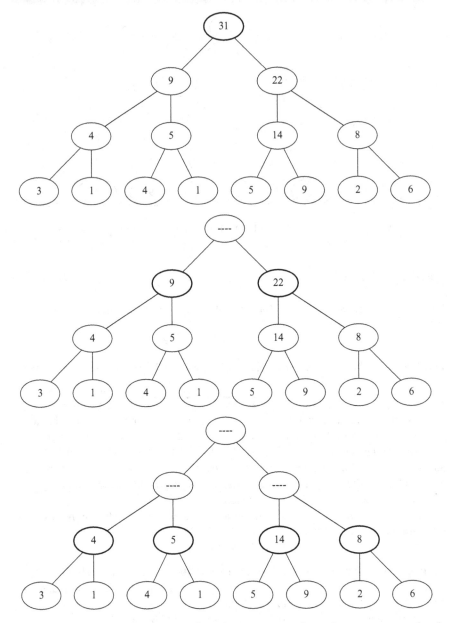

Fig. 3.32: Sum. Trace the progress from *bottom* to *top*. At each step one more level of summations is calculated. This example is small enough that it can be simulated by-hand with people to illustrate the fact that, per level, all calculations may be performed simultaneously in parallel. Powers of two are convenient but not necessary

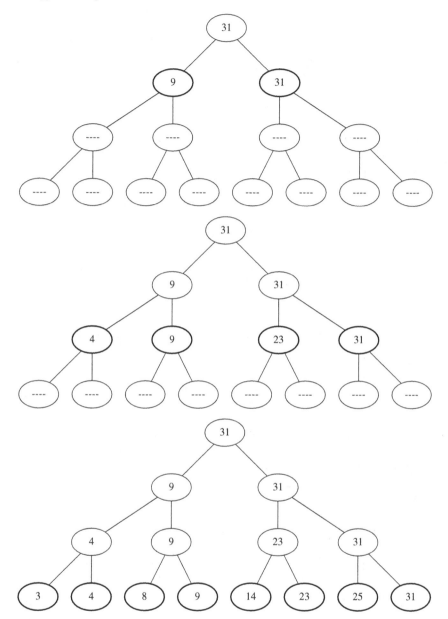

Fig. 3.33: Prefix sum. Now trace the progress from *top* to *bottom* instead. At each step one more level of "prefix sums" is calculated. The set of results at the bottom shows how prefix sum is the "sum so far" of the data, reading from left to right. (Refer to the previous page.) Based upon *Explicit Multi-Threading* by Uzi Vishkin

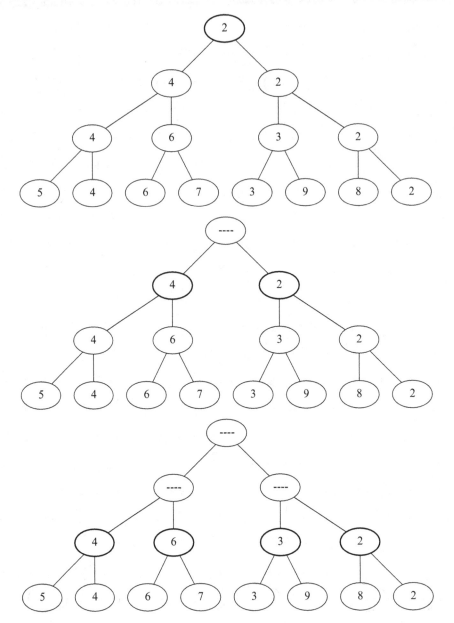

Fig. 3.34: Min. Trace the progress from bottom to top. At each step one more level of minimums is calculated. This example is small enough that it can be simulated by-hand with people to illustrate the fact that, per level, all calculations may be performed simultaneously in parallel. Powers of two are convenient but not necessary

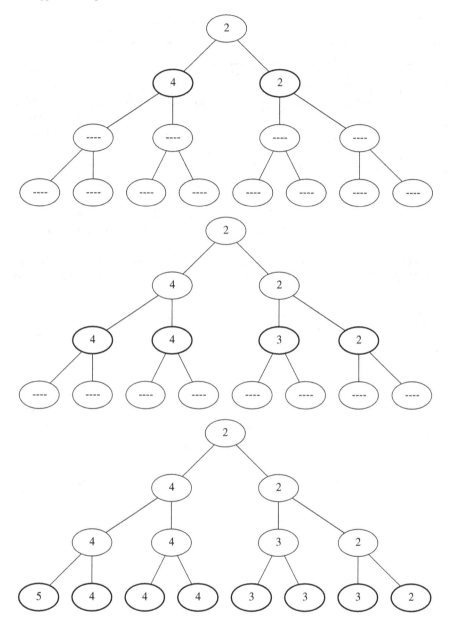

Fig. 3.35: Prefix min. Now trace the progress from top to bottom instead. At each step one more level of "prefix mins" is calculated. The set of results at the bottom shows how prefix min is the "min so far" of the data, reading from left to right. Note that unlike sum, which has subtraction, the min does not have an inverse operation

Table 3.4: Text output of a series converging after only 23 terms

Step, j	Computed π	Current term	$2j-1$	c_{2j-1}	$2^{-(2j-1)}$
1	3.0000000000000000	5.0000e−01	1.0	1.0000	0.500000000000000
2	3.1250000000000000	2.0833e−02	3.0	0.5000	0.125000000000000
3	3.1390625000000001	2.3437e−03	5.0	0.3750	0.031250000000000
4	3.1411551339285717	3.4877e−04	7.0	0.3125	0.007812500000000
5	3.1415111723400302	5.9340e−05	9.0	0.2734	0.001953125000000
22	3.1415926535897936	3.2357e−16	43.0	0.1224	0.0000000000001137
23	3.1415926535897940	**7.5541e−17**	45.0	0.1196	0.0000000000000284
27	3.1415926535897940	2.3067e−19	53.0	0.1101	0.0000000000000001
28	3.1415926535897940	5.4541e−20	55.0	0.1081	0.0000000000000000
530	3.1415926535897940	4.9407e−324	1059.0	0.0245	0.0000000000000000
531	3.1415926535897940	**0.0000e+00**	1061.0	0.0245	0.0000000000000000
math.pi	3.1415926535897931				
$\pi:10^{-16}$	3.1415926535897932				

Lab335: A Better Series

High-quality results in Table 3.4 are based on $\sin 30° = \sin(\pi/6) = 1/2 = x$, and:

$$\frac{\pi}{6} = c_1 x + c_3 \frac{x^3}{3} + c_5 \frac{x^5}{5} + c_7 \frac{x^7}{7} + c_9 \frac{x^9}{9} + c_{11} \frac{x^{11}}{11} + \cdots$$

$$\frac{\pi}{6} = (1)x + \left(c_1 \frac{1}{2}\right)\frac{x^3}{3} + \left(c_3 \frac{3}{4}\right)\frac{x^5}{5} + \left(c_5 \frac{5}{6}\right)\frac{x^7}{7} + \left(c_7 \frac{7}{8}\right)\frac{x^9}{9} + \left(c_9 \frac{9}{10}\right)\frac{x^{11}}{11} + \cdots$$

$$c_1 = 1$$

$$c_3 = \tfrac{1}{2}$$

$$c_5 = \tfrac{1\cdot3}{2\cdot4}$$

$$c_7 = \tfrac{1\cdot3\cdot5}{2\cdot4\cdot6}$$

$$c_9 = \tfrac{1\cdot3\cdot5\cdot7}{2\cdot4\cdot6\cdot8}$$

$$c_{11} = \tfrac{1\cdot3\cdot5\cdot7\cdot9}{2\cdot4\cdot6\cdot8\cdot10}$$

Note how we experience swamping after step 23 long before underflow at step 531.

Chapter 4
Efficiency

To solve a small problem it is unnecessary to write code that runs as fast as possible, but here "small" must be understood reflexively to mean only that a fast running code is not required. Regardless, to solve problems of practical interest it will certainly be necessary that our code runs fast for large cases, and as habits govern so much of our behavior we will do best by writing code for small cases with potential large cases already in mind.

Fig. 4.1: Comparison of runtime efficiency between linear and quadratic algorithms as the size of a problem grows. Small problems appear only in the lower-left corner

© Springer International Publishing 2016

S. Torbert, *Applied Computer Science*, DOI 10.1007/978-3-319-30866-1_4

4.1 Text and Language

Figure 4.1 showed the relative difference in runtime between linear and quadratic algorithms as a problem grows larger and larger. With every order of magnitude increase in problem size the relative difference in runtime grows by *two* orders of magnitude. So if there is a linear solution, find it!

As one example, the Declaration of Independence contains just under 1500 words while Federalist 78 has just over 3000. To determine how many times each unique word appears in these two texts we might use either a linear or quadratic algorithm. On an old PowerPC® chip the linear code ran in 0.009 and 0.02 seconds, respectively, while the quadratic code took 1.1 and 3.9 seconds.

Note that as the problem size doubled the runtime of the linear code also doubled but the quadratic code quadrupled. A fair objection: 4 seconds is not a long time to wait for a code to run regardless of the algorithm. Yet if we consider instead every issue of every newspaper from the past year, or every page of every website from the past 10 years, then *only* the efficiency of our code will matter.

Research in "natural language processing" involves the analysis of these kinds of texts using statistical inference, among other techniques, potentially also studying changes over time. Since understanding requires accurate results (and otherwise what is the point?) it becomes necessary to draw on a very large body of work and this in turn requires a *very* fast running code.

Lab411: Population Cloud

We want to build a word cloud that quickly relays information about the main topics of a work in a visual manner. In preparation, we first build a population cloud for the United States from Census 2000 data as shown in Fig. 4.2.

Code Listing 4.2 shows population data previously used and Code Listing 4.3 shows part of a file to translate from postal abbreviation to full name. Be careful using the `split` function here because some names include more than one word; in fact, this is the reason why the full names are listed on every *other* line of the file, so that `split('\n')` can be used. This will separate the data at newlines only and not at any other whitespace characters.

Your assignment is to display full names, at random positions, where font size is determined by population. Code Listing 4.1 sets the font size of a particular text object from a pre-calculated variable. (Note there is a big lie here: the difference in font size does not reflect the actual difference in, say, Wyoming and California.)

Code Listing 4.1: Setting the font size of a Tk text object from a variable

```
#
cnvs.create_text( ... , font=('Times',fsize,'bold') )
#
```

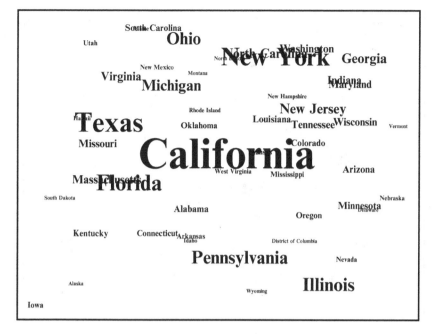

Fig. 4.2: Population cloud based on Census 2000

Code Listing 4.2: Part of the file from Lab314 containing Census 2000 data

```
AL 4447100
AK 626932
AZ 5130632
AR 2673400
CA 33871648
CO 4301261
CT 3405565
. . .
```

Code Listing 4.3: Part of a file to translate from postal abbreviation to full name

```
AL
Alabama
AK
Alaska
AZ
Arizona
. . .
```

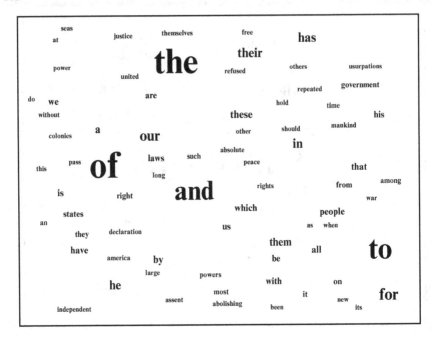

Fig. 4.3: Word cloud where font size is based on relative frequency in the text

Lab412: Word Cloud

Common words such as "of", "the", "to", and "and" make Fig. 4.3 not immediately identifiable with the Declaration of Independence. But, producing this word cloud does require first tabulating the frequency of each unique word in the text, which is a start. Algorithm 4.1.1 shows a quadratic calculation of these frequencies.

Algorithm 4.1.1 Quadratic calculation of word frequencies

1: $words = wordlist$
2: $freq = hashtable$
3: **while** $j = 0, 1, 2, \ldots$ **do**
4:     $count = 0$
5:     **while** $k = 0, 1, 2, \ldots$ **do**
6:         **if** $match$ **then**
7:             $count = count + 1$
8:         **end if**
9:     **end while**
10:     $freq[words[j]] = count$
11: **end while**

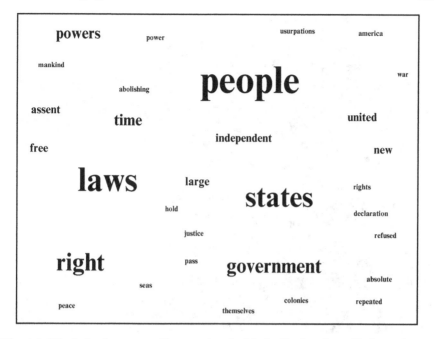

Fig. 4.4: Word cloud more readily associated with the Declaration of Independence, excluding common words and only including words that appear at least three times

Lab413: Uncommon Words

Files of common words can be found on the Internet, or you can build your own. Then, a word cloud like the one shown in Fig. 4.4 may be produced by filtering these words out before (!) tabulating frequencies. Algorithm 4.1.2 outlines an improved linear calculation to count-up each word frequency step-by-step over time.

Algorithm 4.1.2 Linear calculation of word frequencies

1: $words = wordlist$
2: $freq = hashtable$
3: **while** $j = 0, 1, 2, \ldots$ **do**
4:   **if** $first$ **then**
5:     $freq[words[j]] = 1$
6:   **else**
7:     $freq[words[j]] = freq[words[j]] + 1$
8:   **end if**
9: **end while**

Fig. 4.5: Sunset at Cerro Tololo Inter-American Observatory near La Serena, Chile (Image courtesy of the U.S. Navy, photo credit Dr. Brian Mason)

Databases

Accumulation of data continues to grow at a faster-and-faster rate, so much so that researchers in astronomy are now facing issues related to the mere *transfer* of data from observational projects located in Chile, see Fig. 4.5, before analysis can even be performed (i.e., actually doing the science).

However, these problems will be solved because the promise of new learning from massive amounts of data is so attractive. For instance, language translation software that uses computational statistics has become a real alternative to formal linguistics, not in the sense that theory could be abandoned but, as we have seen regarding experiment and computer simulation, theory can be augmented by data.

$$Theory \Leftrightarrow Data$$
$$Experiment \Leftrightarrow Simulation$$

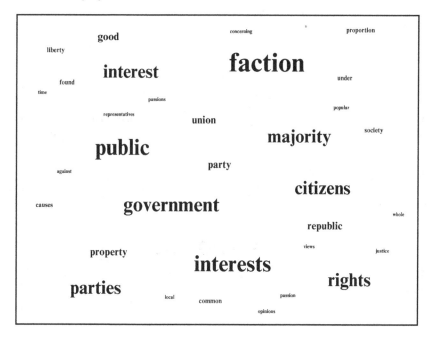

Fig. 4.6: Word cloud from the famous Federalist 10, written by James Madison, shown without overlap between the bounding boxes that surround each word's text

Lab414: Bin Packing

Avoiding overlap requires first finding the width and height of the bounding box that surrounds each word's text. Code Listing 4.4 shows how we might determine these dimensions but still this is a difficult problem related to an even more difficult problem in general: bin packing. Big words are drawn first as it does not get any easier to find a large open space once more-and-more other words have been drawn.

Code Listing 4.4: Text width and height for a specific font and a specific word

```
#
from tkFont import Font
#
f=Font(family='Times',size=fsize,weight='bold')
#
width  = f.measure(the_word)
height = f.metrics()['linespace']
#
```

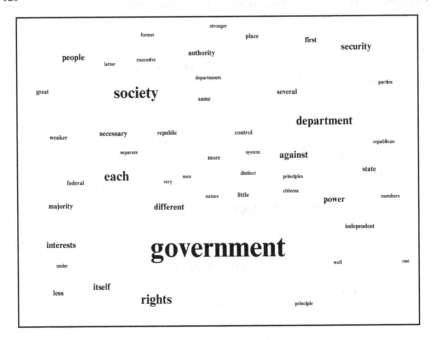

Fig. 4.7: Word cloud from Federalist 51, also written by James Madison

Lab415: Comparison

Comparing the word clouds in Figs. 4.6, 4.7, and 4.8, we see clearly the variety of topics discussed in the Federalist Papers. Keep in mind also that they were written by different people: James Madison, Alexander Hamilton, and John Jay.

   Implement a feature that cycles through all 85 papers showing one cloud on the screen at a time and somehow indicating (background color, footnote) who wrote each article. Note that frequencies of multiple similar words could be combined, too. We might, in this case, count "promise", "promises", "promised", and "promising" as essentially the same word.

In addition, it is okay if the words in your cloud overlap.

   A challenging problem for a computer to solve would be to determine the author from the word cloud but without access to the actual papers themselves, perhaps using only the three authors' other writings as background knowledge.

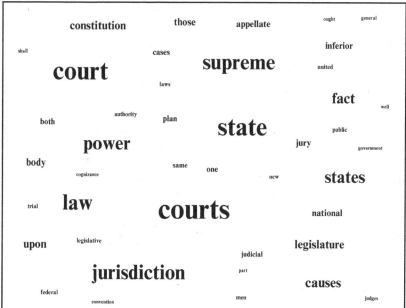

Fig. 4.8: Word clouds from Federalists 78 and 81, written by Alexander Hamilton

Fig. 4.9: Some of the crumbling ruins of ancient Babylon, 1932 (Image courtesy of the G. Eric and Edith Matson Photograph Collection, Library of Congress Prints and Photographs Division, original source American Colony (Jerusalem), Photo Dept)

4.2 Babylonian Method

Figure 4.9 shows the ruins of Babylon in 1932. A clay tablet over 3500 years old depicts their version of Algorithm 4.2.1, a technique now widely used in general. Algebra verifies that Line 3 is equivalent to $x^2 = 2$ but an assignment statement in a computer program is not the same as a mathematical equation; the input and output values will not actually match unless $x = \sqrt{2}$ within machine precision.

Algorithm 4.2.1 Babylonian method for calculating the square root of two

---

1: $x = 5$
2: **while** *changing* **do**
3:    $x = 0.5 \cdot (x + 2/x)$
4:    **print** x
5: **end while**

Lab421: Square Root of Two

Your assignment is to draw a cobweb diagram as shown in Fig. 4.10 where sample output in Code Listing 4.5 displays our sequence of approximations. The solid line in the cobweb diagram is $y = x$ from the left-hand side of Line 3 in Algorithm 4.2.1 and the dashed line is $y = 0.5 \cdot (x + 2/x)$ taken from the right-hand side. Their point of intersection occurs when the input and output values are equal, when $x = \sqrt{2}$.

Code Listing 4.5: A sequence of approximations approaching the square root of two

```
2.7000000000000002
1.7203703703703703
1.4414553681776501
1.4144709813677712
1.4142135857968836
1.4142135623730954
1.4142135623730949
```

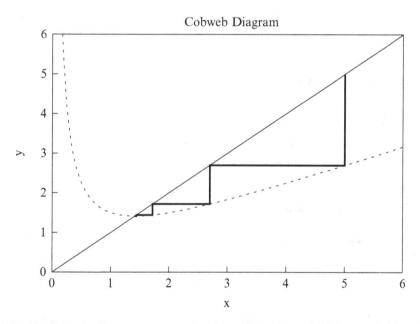

Fig. 4.10: Cobweb diagram, square root of two. Even if our initial guess is absurd the value of x stops changing after only seven steps. A *vertical line* shows how an input produces an output while a *horizontal line* shows how we then use that output as the next input in order to build a sequence of better-and-better approximations

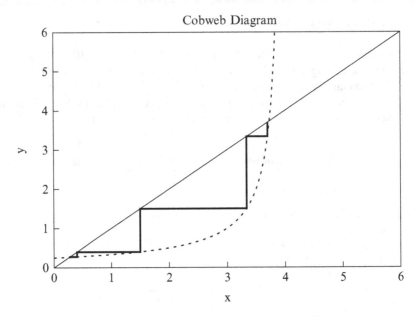

Fig. 4.11: Even though our initial guess is very close to $2 + \sqrt{3} \approx 3.732$ we find the attracting solution at $2 - \sqrt{3} \approx 0.2679$ instead

Lab422: Attract or Repel

Points of intersection on cobweb plots are called "fixed points" because the input-output x is unchanged at these locations. Figure 4.11 uses $x = 1/(4 - x)$ and $x_0 = 3.7$ to solve $0 = x^2 - 4x + 1$ but other schemes are possible and they may be faster or slower than this one; they may also find the other fixed point, too.

An Important Note About Efficiency

Even in cases where a direct method is available (we could have used the quadratic formula, after all) code using an iterative method may run faster, and if our results are sufficiently close that we cannot tell which came from which method then in what sense is the formula more true? Our previous approximation of $\sqrt{2}$ converged to 1.4142135623730949 rather than the value 1.4142135623730951 returned by the math module's sqrt function. Pretty close. Say we were manufacturing a car and needed this calculation; could an industrial saw cut metal with enough precision for the difference to matter? Afterwards, could we even measure the cut metal this precisely? And how does the sqrt function calculate its result anyway?

Fig. 4.12: A gecko climbing up glass. Evidence has suggested that this ability is possible only because an exceedingly large number of very small bristles use intermolecular attraction in a massively parallel way (Image courtesy of Tim Vickers)

Van der Waals

The ideal gas law can, under certain conditions, determine volume V when absolute pressure P, the number of moles n, and absolute temperature T are all known:

$$PV = nRT \quad \Rightarrow \quad V = nRT/P$$

When this fails the following corrections were suggested by van der Waals:

$$\left(P + n^2 a/V^2\right) \cdot (V - nb) = nRT$$

Constants a and b are determined experimentally for particular gases and these added terms account for both intermolecular attraction and the volume of individual particles. (Figure 4.12 shows another practical use of attraction between molecules.) But now how can we solve a cubic equation for V? One option is an iterative method where we use the ideal gas law's solution (!) as our first approximation V_0 and then build a sequence of improved approximations for V from there.

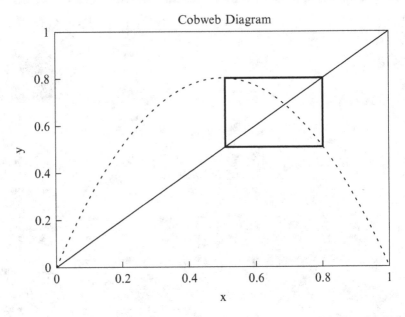

Fig. 4.13: Periodic behavior, oscillation between two points: 0.802 and 0.509

Lab423: Periodic

What happens if our sequence of approximations fails to approach a single value? Figure 4.13 shows just this kind of behavior for $x = 3.21 \cdot x \cdot (1 - x)$ and $x_0 = 0.25$. We run 30 loops first with no display so the values have time to settle down, then show the next 10 loops. Note how an input of 0.802 outputs 0.509, and vice versa.

Lab424: Chaotic

Figure 4.14 shows a very different kind of behavior, chaos, although the only change is now $x = 3.99 \cdot x \cdot (1 - x)$ and $x_0 = 0.25$. Systems that are this sensitive to slight variations in a model parameter occur most famously in weather forecasting where the so-called "butterfly effect" discovered by Lorenz makes it difficult to predict events beyond the very short term. (As the story goes, a butterfly flapping its wings in San Francisco causes a rainstorm to develop later in New Jersey.)

Code Listing 4.6 shows sample output after $O\left(10^4\right)$ loops, seemingly a sufficient amount of time for any transient movement to have ended and yet still no regular pattern has emerged between any number of points.

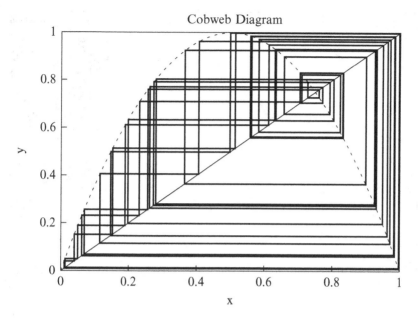

Fig. 4.14: Chaotic behavior, no regular pattern emerges over time

Code Listing 4.6: A sequence that fails to "settle down" over time

```
    :
0.8032323382113545
0.6306200947608700
0.9294241794701987
0.2617235476045228
0.7709650856129653
0.7045459102912460
0.8305622726266709
0.5615070498244030
0.9824053624593747
0.0689674144190529
0.2562015315679398
0.7603436040928253
0.7270626191537534
0.7917858422623198
0.6577954787985217
0.8981513416142737
```

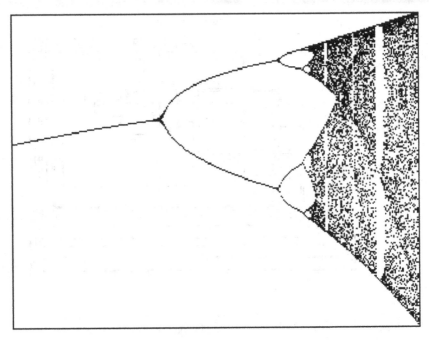

Fig. 4.15: Logistic map, a one-parameter system, shown for $r = 2.4$ to $r = 4$

Lab425: Logistic Map

Figure 4.15 shows a general iterative scheme $x = r \cdot x \cdot (1 - x)$ as we vary r. In all cases $x_0 = 0.25$ to start. This is known as the logistic map and we might think of our vertical scale as the population of deer, for instance, changing in response to r, which could represent an environmental condition of some kind. Please do not be troubled by the fact that this x now relates to yp in the graphics window:

$$xp \Leftrightarrow r$$

$$yp \Leftrightarrow x$$

At left we see a stable population, first at a constant value increasing with r and later periodic after the so-called "bifurcation" where the population then oscillates between two, four, or eight values. These periodic regions might represent cyclic changes in our deer population, from either seasonal or migratory effects perhaps, but they are stable nevertheless. The bifurcation points themselves would appear even sharper if more pre-drawing loops were used. At right we see... chaos.

Code Listing 4.7 shows how to animate this plot. It is easier to change xp at each step and interpolate from there to r than the other way around. Also, drawing very small 1×1 rectangles for each pixel is too slow so we use a PIL image instead.

Code Listing 4.7: Shell for part of a program

```
...
#
img=Image.new('RGB',(w,h),(255,255,255))
pmg=ImageTk.PhotoImage(img)
#
# a single Tk image object is drawn...
#
tkid=cnvs.create_image(w/2,h/2,image=pmg)
#
def tick():
    global xp,pmg
    #
    # no loop for xp, rather... animation with tick/if
    #
    if xp<w:
        #
        r=rmin+xp*(rmax-rmin)/w   # interpolate
        #
        x=0.25
        #
        ...
        #
        t=0
        while t<100:
            #
            ...
            #
            yp=int(h-h*x)
            img.putpixel((xp,yp),(0,0,0))
            #
            t+=1
        #
        # photo image object must be global
        #
        pmg=ImageTk.PhotoImage(img)
        cnvs.itemconfigure(tkid,image=pmg)
        #
        xp+=1
        #
    #
    cnvs.after(1,tick)
#
...
```

Moment of Reflection

Code Listing 4.8 shows how to produce Fig. 4.10 previously shown. The vertical
and horizontal segments are specified by the output file shown in Code Listing 4.9.
Both the left- and right-hand side of the iterative scheme have been drawn explicitly,
one solid line by `lt -1` and the other dashed by `lt 0`.

It is important that you pause regularly to review your own code. Go back and
read what you wrote, compare your approach to others, talk to people about how
you are thinking though a problem.

Even if they cannot follow the technical details, the process of activating your
mind to formulate an explanation for someone else will be helpful. And remember
the importance of commenting your code because often the next person to read it
will be your own future self. You will appreciate those comments later!

Code Listing 4.8: Gnuplot command to draw a cobweb diagram

```
plot "lab421.txt"  w l notitle lt -1 lw 2, \
     x             w l notitle lt -1 lw 1, \
     0.5*(x+2.0/x) w l notitle lt  0 lw 3
```

Code Listing 4.9: Sample output in cobweb diagram format

```
5.0 5.0
5.0 2.7
2.7 2.7
2.7 1.72037037037
1.72037037037 1.72037037037
1.72037037037 1.44145536818
1.44145536818 1.44145536818
1.44145536818 1.41447098137
. . .
```

A Useful Insight

After four steps our approximation is:

$$1.41447098137^2 = 2.000728157137811$$

Subsequent improvements are not visible in the cobweb diagram and most likely
represent a sub-pixel distinction. Earlier we stopped our sequence of approximations
when the value stored in a double-precision float would no longer change.

If our ultimate goal is a plot, however, we could have stopped as soon as the
pixels *themselves* no longer changed.

No Animation

Lab425 combined ideas from Lab131 and Lab211. If no animation is desired then Code Listing 4.10 shows a simpler approach. The output PNG file was converted into EPS format using the ImageMagick® command:

```
convert lab425.png lab425.eps
```

Later we will use this same tool to build an animated GIF from the individual frames of a movie, after our program has finished running, as a post-processing step.

Code Listing 4.10: Almost an entire program with no animation

```
#
rmin,rmax=2.4,4.0
#
img=Image.new('RGB',(w,h),(255,255,255))
#
xp=0
#
while xp<w:
        #
        r=rmin+xp*(rmax-rmin)/w   # interpolate
        #
        x=0.25
        #
        t=0
        while t<100:               # settle down
                x=r*x*(1.0-x)
                t+=1
        #
        t=0
        while t<100:               # now display
                x=r*x*(1.0-x)
                #
                yp=int(h-h*x)
                #
                img.putpixel((xp,yp),(0,0,0))
                #
                t+=1
        #
        xp+=1
#
img.save('lab425.png')
#
```

4.3 Workload Balance

Consider a similar iterative scheme but now in 2-D using complex numbers:

$$z = x + yi$$
$$i = \sqrt{-1}$$

Except for the rare historical genius it was only the latter half of the last century when computers allowed humans to even *see* the structures these schemes generate.

Lab431: Three Test Cases

We investigate the general sequence:

$$z_0 = 0$$
$$z = z^2 + c$$

First calculate the constant term $c = c_1 + c_2 i$ from (xp, yp) screen coordinates and then update $z = x + yi$ with:

$$x = x^2 - y^2 + c_1$$
$$y = 2xy + c_2$$

Even though complex numbers are used in this formulation our code will only involve real numbers; but now two, x and y, instead of one. Code Listing 4.11 shows three test cases and we want to know if each sequence is "well-behaved" or not, meaning that convergence to a single value, periodic oscillation, *and* chaotic behavior are all treated the same.

On the other hand unbounded growth (such a case is said to "blow up") is of particular interest, and we note how many steps it takes to explode. Observation indicates that if at any step $\sqrt{x^2 + y^2} \geq 2$ then the sequence will not behave and so we can give up immediately. Otherwise we wait until 100 steps to stop the loop.

Code Listing 4.11: Three test cases for an iterative scheme using complex numbers

```
c1=-0.625 converges
c2=-0.250

c1= 0.375 blows up at step 17
c2=-0.375

c1= 0.375 chaotic?
c2=-0.250
```

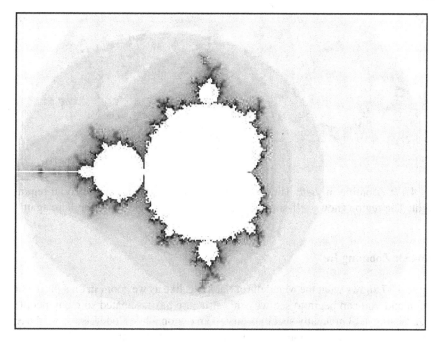

Fig. 4.16: The famous Mandelbrot Set

Lab432: Mandelbrot Set

Use code similar to our animated plot of the logistic map. Again xp is updated at each step but its value is now associated with c_1 rather than r, and within `tick` we loop over all yp and each value is translated to c_2. Figure 4.16 shows our plot, drawn column-by-column. Color each pixel based on the number of steps its associated sequence makes before blowing up. Code Listing 4.12 shows how to get a color value from the loop count assuming some maximum number of loops (e.g., 100).

Code Listing 4.12: Some commands to help generate and plot the Mandelbrot Set

```
xmin,xmax=-2.0,2.0
ymin,ymax=-1.5,1.5
#
c1=xmin+xp*(xmax-xmin)/w
c2=ymax+yp*(ymin-ymax)/h # inverted
#
value=(1.0-count/100.0)**3.0
color=int(255.0*value+0.5)
```

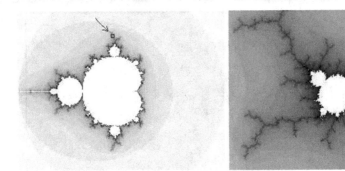

Fig. 4.17: Zooming in. *Left*: The arrow points to a box indicating the zoom region. Right: The region shows self-similarity as the original shape is present here again

Lab433: Zooming In

Figure 4.17 shows what the Mandelbrot Set looks like as we zoom in on a particular region and you can begin to see why this structure has fascinated so many people. Code Listing 4.13 manually specifies this zoom region while Code Listing 4.14 uses mouse clicks in order to zoom interactively, reducing both x and y by a factor of 2.

Code Listing 4.13: Manually specifying the zoom region

```
#
xmin=-0.18984375
xmax=-0.12734375
ymin= 1.010546875
ymax= 1.057421875
#
```

Code Listing 4.14: Using mouse clicks to zoom interactively

```
#
# click is at (xc,yc)
#
dx=0.5*(xmax-xmin)
dy=0.5*(ymax-ymin)
#
xmin=xc-0.5*dx
xmax=xc+0.5*dx
ymin=yc-0.5*dy
ymax=yc+0.5*dy
#
```

Fig. 4.18: Zooming and sharpening. *Left*: Zoom region taken from upper-left quadrant of previous zoom region. *Right*: Doubling of iteration count sharpens features

Parallel Load Balancing

In the special case of interactive zooming we must be careful not to draw the image too inefficiently. For instance, if the putpixel command is placed inside our inner-most loop, and if itemconfigure is placed inside any loop, then runtime may increase by three (!) orders of magnitude. It may run 1,000 times slower!

Also, if we zoom in on a small enough region then we will need to increase the maximum iteration count so that the details of our plot do not become smeared, shown in Fig. 4.18. Doubling of the iteration count from 100 to 200 increases our overall runtime roughly by a factor of two. In particular those sequences that do not blow up will necessarily loop for the maximum count. Code Listing 4.15 manually specifies this zoom region. On the next few pages Figs. 4.19, 4.20, and 4.21 show zoom regions with a variety of other "interesting" features.

Code Listing 4.15: Manually specifying the zoom region

```
#
xmin=-0.167883300781
xmax=-0.166906738281
ymin= 1.04083862305
ymax= 1.04157104492
#
```

This is an embarrassingly parallel problem and we can use spatial decomposition to assign different columns to different parallel nodes, but not all columns are equal in terms of workload. Those columns with more pixels whose corresponding sequence is well-behaved (these are actually the only points *in* the Mandelbrot Set) will require more time than those with many sequences that blow up quickly.

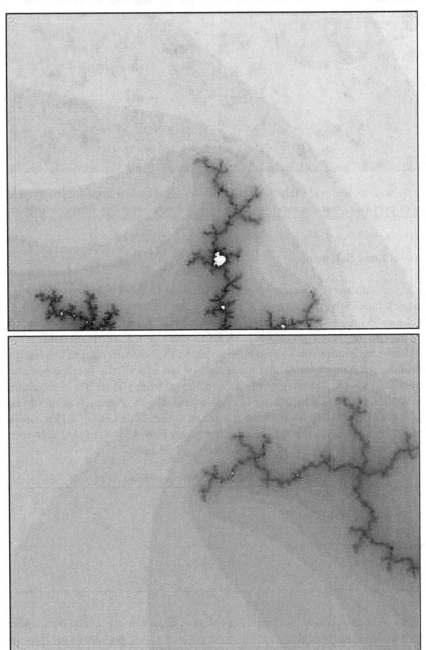

Fig. 4.19: Spiral, located along the upper-right edge of the overall set, as we zoom further-and-further the spiral turns round-and-round, seemingly forever. *Top*: spiral with "tip" first pointing up and left, turning counterclockwise. *Bottom*: the same spiral zoomed-in more so that the tip is now pointing left and down

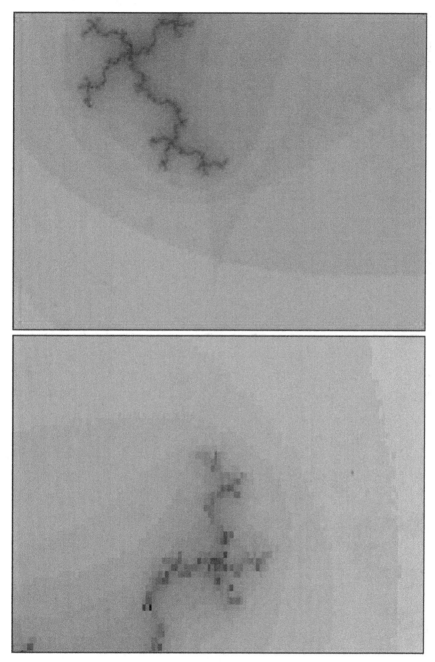

Fig. 4.20: Spiral, if we zoom in far enough the image will pixelate once the floating-point values are sufficiently close together. *Top*: same as before but now pointing down and right. *Bottom*: a few "full" spins later our spiral has become pixelated; note that intensities have been artificially enhanced to sharpen the details

Fig. 4.21: More features. *Top*: a "valley" between the overall "head" and "body". *Bottom*: zoomed further, one of many tendril-like "flowers" present in this valley

Lab434: Movie

We make a "movie" of the Mandelbrot Set by zooming in, see Code Listing 4.16, then panning across that image. Code Listing 4.17 shows left to right motion where only the end-column is calculated for our next image; all the others just shift over, thus saving a factor of $O(100)$, i.e. the max iteration count, a comparable speed-up to rendering on a 100-node parallel system, only cheaper! Each image is saved as a separate PNG file with frames numbered from 000 to 999, and once we have all the frames they can be combined together into a single animated GIF file:

```
convert -delay 10 -loop 1 frame*.png movie.gif
```

In only minutes a program of size 3.4 KB is generating files of total size 15 MB, a factor of over 4,000. Wow!

Code Listing 4.16: Manually specifying the zoom region

```
#
xmin=-2.0
xmax=-1.0
ymin=-0.0625
ymax= 0.6875
#
```

Code Listing 4.17: Incremental updates as we pan across a zoomed image

```
#
img.save('frame%03d.png'%frame) # 1000 frames
frame+=1
#
xp=0
while xp<w-1:
    yp=0
    while yp<h:
        #
        red,green,blue=img.getpixel((xp+1,yp)) # shift
        img.putpixel((xp,yp),(red,green,blue))
        #
        yp+=1
    xp+=1
#
# xp==w-1, the one new column we now need to render
#
xmin += ...
xmax += ...
```

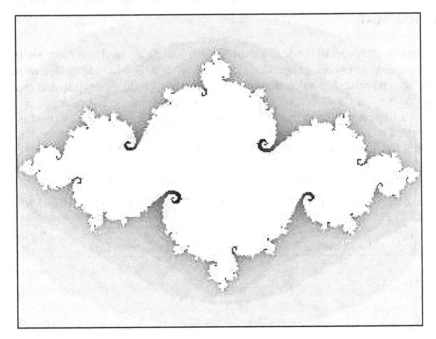

Fig. 4.22: An example Julia Set closely related to the Mandelbrot Set

Lab435: Julia Sets

We can generate any number of so-called Julia Sets by first fixing c_1 and c_2 then using (xp, yp) to initialize x and y, instead of zero (i.e., no longer initialize $z_0 = 0$). One such plot is shown in Fig. 4.22, see also Code Listing 4.18, but others are possible. We can build a movie by displaying a sequence of these Julia Sets and frame-to-frame transitions will be "interesting" if the corresponding c-values mark a continuous path, particularly from along the Mandelbrot Set's edge. Such a movie based on our plot here might show the "spikes" waving back-and-forth over time.

Code Listing 4.18: Some commands to help generate and plot a Julia Set

```
xmin,xmax=-1.500,1.500
ymin,ymax=-1.125,1.125
#
c1=-0.7375 # fixed
c2= 0.0625
#
x0=xmin+xp*(xmax-xmin)/w
y0=ymax+yp*(ymin-ymax)/h
```

Chapter 5
Recursion

First, recursion will necessarily involve the use of a function, always.

Second, that function will make at least one recursive call *to itself*.

Third, even if this seems strange Fig. 5.1 shows one of the many practical applications of recursion. Shortly of course, we will see more.

Fourth, if you find this unconvincing then you should read it all again starting from the second sentence. Otherwise, turn to the next page.

Fig. 5.1: A scene in 3-D rendered using recursive ray tracing, where reflections appear within reflections of their own reflections (Image courtesy of Al Hart)

© Springer International Publishing 2016

S. Torbert, *Applied Computer Science*, DOI 10.1007/978-3-319-30866-1_5

5.1 Disease Outbreak

Imagine a group of people who all come in close contact on a regular basis. It may be
the case that Alice never comes in contact with Bob but instead they both contact the
same third-person, Eve, so that if any one of the three should become sick it would
be possible for the illness to travel (directly or indirectly) to each of the others.

Lab511: Initial Conditions

We begin with random initialization of a 2-D grid to establish the social relationships
described above. We use a 1-D list to represent this grid and translate back-and-forth
between list index and (x, y) grid coordinates as shown in Code Listings 5.1 and 5.2.
Results for $p = 0.6$ and $p = 0.7$ are shown in Code Listing 5.3 on the next page.

Code Listing 5.1: Randomly initializing a 1-D list

```
j=0
while j<len(grid):
    #
    r=random()
    #
    if r<0.1:
        grid[j]='X' # sick
    elif r<p:
        grid[j]='O' # healthy
    #
    j+=1
#
```

Code Listing 5.2: Printing a 1-D list as a 2-D grid

```
y=0
while y<h:
    x=0
    while x<w:
        #
        j=y*w+x        # translate from 2-D to 1-D
        #
        print grid[j],
        x+=1
    print
    y+=1
print
#
```

Code Listing 5.3: Random grids. Empty slots are shown as dashes, healthy people as 'O', and sick people as 'X' (also in bold). Top: 40 % empty. Bottom: 30 % empty

```
O - X O O - X - O X O O O O - - O O O O - - O O O - O O - O O O X O O X - O - -
O O O - O - O - O O O X - X O - O O - - O X - O - O X X - X - O O O - O O - O O
X O O O O - O - - - - - O - - O O - O - O O - O - O - - O O O - X - - O - O O O
O O O - O - O O O - - - O O O - X O O - O X O O O O O O O O - - ' - - - O - O X
- O - O - - - O O X X O - O O X O - O - - O O O X O - O O O O - X - - - -
O X X O - O O O - - O O O - - - - O - X - O O O - O X - - O - O O - O O - O O O
O - O O O - - - O - O - - O - - O O - O O O - O O - O O - O O O O O O O O - - -
O O - O O - O O O O X O O - - - O O - O - - X - O - - O - - O O X O O O - O O O
O X - - O - O O O - - O O - O X O O - X - - O O O O - O O - O - O O O - O O O
O - - - - O - - - - O O O O O - O O O X - X O - O - O - O - O O O - - - - O O
- - O - O - O O X - - - O O - - X O O O O - - - O O O O O - O O - O O - O O - O
O - O - X O O - - - O O O - - O O - - O O O O - - O - - O O X O O O - O X - - O
X - - X O O O - O - - O - - - - - O O O X O - O - O O O O O X O - - O - O -
X - O O - O - X O - O - - X O - O - - O - X - X O O - X O O - O O O - O O O - O
X O - O O - O O - - - - X X - - X O - O - O - - O O - O - O O - - O X O O O O O
O O O - O - X O - O O O O O O O X O - X O O - O O O - O - X - O O O X O O O -
O O O - O O - - - O O O - O O O - O O - - O O O - X O - O X O - X - - X O
X O - O O O - X O - O X O X X X O - - O O O - O X O O X - O O O - O X O O O O -
- X - X X O O - O - O O X - - - - O O - O O - X O O O O O O O O O O O - - X O O -
O O O - O O O - - - - - O - O - - - O - O O O O - O X - O O - O - - - O O - X O
O O O - - - - O - O O O O X - - O - - - O O X - - - - - O O O - X - O -
O - O - O - X - O X O - O O X O - - O O O X X O O O O - - - - - - - O - - - - O
O - - O O O - - - - O X O - O - - - - - - O O - O - - O - O - - - X O - - - O
- O - - O - O O - - - O O O - - O - X O - O X X O O - O X - - O - O O O O - O O -
O O O O O - O - - - O - O - O - O O O - - - O - O - - - - O O O O - X - X O O - -
- O - - O O X X O X - O X - O - O - - - - O X - O - O - O O - - O - O O - O
O O O O O O O X - O X - X O - O - - - O - O O X O O O X O X - O O O X X - - - X
X X O O O - O O X - O O O - O X - - O O - O X X O - X O O X X O - - O O - - - O
O O O O - O O X O X O O O - - - - O O O O O O O O O O O - - - - - O - - - O O
O - X O - X O X - - O O O O O - - O O X O - X X O O - - - - O - - X O - - O O O
```

```
O O X O O O X - O X O O O O - O O O O O - - O O O - O O O O O O X O O X - O - O
O O O - O - O - O O O X - X O O O O - - O X - O O O X X - X O O O O - O O - O O
X O O O O - O - - - O - O - - O O - O - O O - O - O - O - O O O O - X O - O - O O O
O O O - O O O O O O - - - O O O - X O O - O X O O O O O O O O - O O - - O - O X
- O - O - - - O O X X O - O O X O - O - - O O O X O - - O O O O - X - - - -
O X X O - O O O - O O O O - - - - O O - X - O O O - O X - - O - O O - O O - O O O
O - O O O O - - O - O - - O - - O O - O O O - O O - O O - O O O - O O O O O O - - -
O O - O O - O O O O X O O O - O O O - O - - X - O - - O O - - O O X O O O - O O O
O X - - O O - O O O - - O O - O X O O - X - - O O O O - O O O O O O O O O - O O -
O - O - - O O - - O O O O O O O O O X - X O - O - O - O - O O O O - - - - O - O O
O O O - - O - O O X - - - O O O - X O O O O - O - O O O O O - O O O - O O - O O -
O - O - X O O - O - O O O - - O O - - O O O O O O - - O O X O O O - O X O - O
X O O X O O O - O - - O - - - - - O O O X O - O - O O O O O X O O - O O - O -
X - O O - O - X O O O - - X O - O - O - - O - X - O - O - O - O O O - O X O O O O O
X O - O O - O O - - - - X X O - X O - O - O - O - - O O - O - O O O O O X O O O O O
O O O - O - X O O O O O O O O O X O - X O O O - O O O - O - X - O O O X O O O O
O O O O O O - - O O O O - O O O - O O - - O O O - X O O X O - X - O X - O X O
X O O O O O - X O - O X O X X X O - O O O O - O O O O O X O O O O O O O O O O O -
- X O X X O O - O O O O X - O - O O O - O O - X O O O O O O O O O O O O O - - X O O -
O O O - O O O O O - O - O - O - - - O O O O O O X - O O - O - O - O O O O O X O
O O O - - - O O O O O O O X - - O - - - O O X - O O - O O O - O O O O O X O O - -
O - O O - O - X - O X O O O O X O - - O O O X X O O O O - O - - O - O - O - O O
O O - O O O O - - - O X O O O - O - - O O O O - O - - O - O - - - X O O - O O O
- O - - O - O O - - - O O O - - O X O O O X X O O - O X O O O - O O O O O - O O -
O O O O O - O - O - - O O O O - O O O - - - O - O - - O - O O O - X O X O O - -
O O - - O O X X O X - O X - O X O O O O O - O O O O O O - O O - O O O O O - O -
O O O O O O O X - O X - X O - O O - O O - O O X O O O X O X - O O O X X - - - X
X X O O O - O O X - O O O - O X O - O O O O X X O O X O O X X O - - O O - - - O
O O O O - O O X O X O O O - O - - O O O O O O O O O O O O - - - - O - - - O O
O O X O - X O X O - O O O O O - O O O X O - X X O O O - O - O - - X O O - O O O
```

Code Listing 5.4: Infection. Top: Same 40 % empty grid. Bottom: Once-healthy
nearest neighbors of everyone initially marked as sick are now also sick themselves

```
o - X o o - X - o X o o o o - - o o o o - - o o o - o o - o o o X o o X - o - -
o o o - o - o - o o o X - X o - o o - - o X - o - o X X - X - o o o - o o - o o
X o o o o - o - - - - - o - - o o - o - o o - o - o - - o o o - X - - o - o o o
o o o - - o - o o o - - - o o o - X o - o X o o o o o o o o - - - - - o - o o X
- o - o - - o - o - o o X X o - o o X o - o - - o o o X o - o o o o - X - - - -
o X X o - o o o - - o o o - - o - - o - X - o o o - o X - - o - o o - o o - o o o
o - o o o - - - o - o - - o - - o o - o o o - o o o - o o - - o o o o o o o - - -
o o - o o - o o o o X o o - - - o - o - - X - o - - o - - o o X o o o - o o o
o X - - o - o - o o - - o o - o X o o - X - - o o o o - o o - o - o o o - o o -
o - - - - o - - - - o o o o - o o o X - X o - o - o - o - o o o - - - - - o o
- - o - - o - o o X - - - o o - - X o o o o - - - o o o o - o o o - o o o - o -
o - o - X o o - - - o o o - - o o - - o o o - - o - o - o o - X o o o - o X - - o
X - - X o o o - o - - o - - - - - - o o o X o - o - o o o o o X o - - o - o -
X - o o - o - X o - o - - X o - o - o - X - X o o - X o o - o o o - o - - o o
X o - o o - o o - - - - X X - - X o - o - o - - o o - o - o o - - o X o o o o o
o o o - o - X o - o o o o o o o X o - X o o - - - o o o - o - X - o o o X o o o -
o o o - o o o - - - - o - - o o - o o - o o o - - o - X o - o X o - X - - X o
X o - o o o - X o - o X o X X X o - - o o o - o X o o X - o o o - o X o o o o -
- X - X X o o - o - o o X - - - - o o - o o - o - X o o o o o o o o o o - - X o o -
o o o - o o o - - - - - o - o - - o - o o o o - o X - o o - o - - - o o - X o
o o o - - - - o - - o o o o X - o - - - - o o X - - - - - o o o - X - o - -
o - o - - o - X - o X o - o o X o - - o o o X X o o o o - - o - - - - - o - o
o - - o o o - - - - o X o - o - - - - - - o o - o - - o - o - - - X o - - - o
- o - - o - o o - - - o o o - - o - X o - o X X o o - o X - - o - o o o o - o o -
o o o o o - o - - - - o - o - o - o o o - - o - o - - o o o o - X - X o o - -
- o - - o o X X o X - o X - o - - o - - o o X - - o - o o o - o o o o o o o
o o o o o o o X - o X - X o - o - o - - - o - o o X o o o X o X - o o o X X - - - X
X X o o o - o o X - o o o - o X - - o o - o X X o - X o o X X o - - o o - - - o
o o o o - o o X o X o o o - - - - o o o o o o o o o o o o - - - - o - - - o o
o - X o - X o X - - o o o o o - - o o X o - X X o o - - - - o - - X o - - o o o
```

```
o - X X o - X - X X X X o X - - o o o o - - o o o - X X - X o X X X X X - o - -
X o X - o - X - o X X X - X X - o o - - X X - o - X X X - X - o X o - X o - o o
X X o o o - o - - - - - o - - o o - o - o X - o - o - - o X o - X - - o - o o X
X o o - - o - o o o - - - o o o - X X o - X X X o o X o o o o - - - - - o - X X
- X - o - - - o o X X X X - o X X X X o - o X X X - - - o o o o o - X - - - -
X X X X - o o o - - o X X - - X - X - o - o o - X X - - o - o o - o X o o o - o o o
o - X o o - - - o - X - - o - - o o - X o o - o o - o X o - - o o X o o o o - - -
o X - o o - o o o X X X o - - - X o - o - - X - o - - o - - o o X X o o o - o o o
X X - - o - o - o o - - o o X X X o - X - - o o o o - o o - o - o o o - o o -
o - - - - o - - - - o o o o - X X X X - X X - X X - o - o - o o o - - - - - o o
- - o - - o - o X X - - - o o - - X X X o X - - - o o o o o - o o o - o X - o -
X - o - X X o - - - o o o - - o o - - o o o X - - o - o - X X X o o - X X - - o
X - - X X o - o - - o - - X X - X - o - X - X X o o - X X o - X o o o - o - - o o
X X - o o - X X - - - - X X - - X X - o - X - o X - o o - o - o X - o X - - X X X
X o o - o - X X - o o o X X o X X X - X X o - - o o o - o - o o - - X X X X X o X -
X o o - o - - - o o X o - X X X - o - X X X - o X - o o X - o o o - o X - X o X X o X -
X X - X X o - X X - X X X X X X X X - - - o o o - X X X X X - o o o - X X X X o X -
- X - X X X o - o - o o X X - - - - o o - o o - X X o X X o o o o o o - - X X X -
o X o - X o o - - - - - X - X - - - o - o o o X - X X - o o - o - - - X X - X X
o o o - - - - o - - X o o o X X - o - - - - o o X X X o o o o - - - - - o - o - - o
o - o - - o - X - o X X X - o X X X - - o o X X X X o o o o - - o - - - - - o - o
o - - o o o - - X X X - o - - - - - - o o X X - o - - o - o - - - X X - - - o
- o - - o - o o - - o X o - - o X X - X X X X X o - X X - - o - X o X o - o o -
o o o o o - X - - - - o - o - o - o X o - - X - o - - X o o o - X - X o o - -
- o - X X X X X - X X - o X - o - - o - - o X X - - o - o X - - X o X - o X X o o o X
X X o o o o X X - X X - X X - X - - o - o X X X o X X X X - o o X X X - - - X
X X X o o - o X X - X o X - X X - - o o - X X X X - X X X X X X - - X X - - - X
X X X o - X X X X X X o o - - - - o o X o o X X o o X o o X o o - - - - - o - - - o o
o - X X - X X X - - o o o o o - - o X X X - X X X o - - - - o - - X X - - o o o
```

Lab512: Nearest Neighbors

Imagine now that all the sick people cough. Assume that everyone standing directly next to this cough becomes infected. These neighbors are not sick right away but they will be shortly. Consider only the four directions up, down, left, and right.

Regarding the *spread* of disease this represents just a single step. The sick people have coughed on their neighbors but those neighbors have not yet coughed on their neighbors... so the neighbor's neighbor may not be sick (for now). Code Listing 5.4 on the previous page shows output for the same grid initialization as before.

Watch out for the common error of looping low to high and thus cascading the disease farther to the right and down than you really mean to. In the next lab we will do exactly that *on purpose* and in all four directions. Code Listing 5.5 shows the sick (maybe) infecting their neighbors, if the neighboring slot is even in bounds.

Code Listing 5.5: The sick infecting only (!) their nearest neighbors

```
#
def maybe_infect(grid,x,y):
    if 0<=x<w and 0<=y<h:       # Are we even in bounds?
        j=y*w+x
        if grid[j]!='-':        # Is this an empty slot?
            if grid[j]!='X':    # Are we already sick?
                grid[j]='*'     # Mark "going to be sick."
#
j=0
while j<w*h:
    if grid[j]=='X':
        #
        y=j/w                   # translate from 1-D to 2-D
        x=j%w
        #
        maybe_infect(grid,x,y-1) # up
        maybe_infect(grid,x,y+1) # down
        maybe_infect(grid,x-1,y) # left
        maybe_infect(grid,x+1,y) # right
        #
    j+=1
#
# Convert the "going to be sick" into actually sick.
#
j=0
while j<w*h:
    if grid[j]=='*': grid[j]='X'
    j+=1
#
```

Lab513: Floodfill

Imagine the coughing is uncontrollable. Everyone sick is coughing and everyone they cough on gets sick. Soon the entire social circle is sick and since the newly-sick are immediately coughing on their once-healthy neighbors we no longer need to use the asterisk (∗) to mark anyone as "going to be sick." They are all just sick, right away... thank goodness disease doesn't actually spread this fast!

Code Listing 5.7 on the next page shows the expected output, again for the same grid initialization (go back and compare to see for yourself). Code Listing 5.6 shows how to *recursively* infect the neighbor's neighbor's neighbor, and so on.

Code Listing 5.6: Floodfill. Sick people infecting everyone else in their social circle

```
#
def maybe_infect(grid,x,y):
    if 0<=x<w and 0<=y<h:      # Are we even in bounds?
        j=y*w+x
        if grid[j]!='-':        # Is this an empty slot?
            if grid[j]!='X':    # Are we already sick?
                grid[j]='X'     # Mark as sick.
                #
                # recursion...
                #
                maybe_infect(grid,x,y-1) # up
                #
                # recursion...
                #
                maybe_infect(grid,x,y+1) # down
                #
                # recursion...
                #
                maybe_infect(grid,x-1,y) # left
                #
                # recursion...
                #
                maybe_infect(grid,x+1,y) # right
#
```

In this code it is essential that we "mark as sick" immediately because otherwise the recursion will go back-and-forth between neighbors, each infecting the other over and over and over again until we reach the depth limit (typically 1000 calls).

The condition that a person is *already* sick is known as the "base case" and this is what stops the sequence of recursive calls from continuing. After all, there are only so many slots in the grid and thus only so many healthy people to infect.

In general this algorithm is known as "floodfill" and it could also be used to implement a fill-the-area tool in our drawing program from Chap. 2.

Code Listing 5.7: Recursive infection. Top: Again, same 40 % empty grid as before. Bottom: Everyone in the social circle of a sick person is now sick themselves, too

```
O - X O O - X - O X O O O O - - O O O O - - O O O - O O - O O O X O O X - O - -
O O O - O - O - O O O X - X O - O O - - O X - O - O X X - X - O O O - O O - O O
X O O O O - O - - - - - O - - O O - O - O O - O - O - - O O O - X - - O - O O O
O O O - - O - O O O - - - O O O - X O O - O X O O O O O O O - - - - - O - O X
- O - O - - - O - O O X X O - O O X O - O - - - O O O X O - - O O O O - X - - - -
O X X O - O O O - - O O O - - - - O - X - O O O - O X - - O - O O - O O - O O O
O - O O O - - - O - O - - O - - O O - O O O - O O - O O - - O O O O O O O - - -
O O - O O - O O O O X O O - - - O O - O - - X - O - - O - O O X O O O - O O O
O X - - O - O O O - - O O - O X O O - X - - O O O O - O O - O - O O O - O O -
O - - - - O - - - - O O O O - O O O X - X O - O - O - O - O - O O O - - - - O O
- - O - O - O O X - - - O O - - X O O O O - - - O O O O O - O O O - - O O - O -
O - O - X O - - O O O - - O O - - O O - - O O O O - O O O X O O O - O X - - O
X - - X O O O - O - - O - - - - O O O X O - O O O O O O X O - - O - O -
X - O O - O - X O - O - - X O - O - - O - X - X O O - X O O - O O O - O - O -
X O - O O - O O - - - - X X - - X O - O - O - - O O - O - O O - - O X O O O O O
O O O - - O - X O - O O O O O O O X O - X O O - - - O O O - O - X - - O O X O O O
O O O - O O - - O - O O O O - O O O - O O O - - O - X O - O X O - X O - - X O
X O - O O O - X O - O X O X X X O - - O O O - O X O O X - O O O - O X O O O O -
- X - X X O O - O - - O O X - - - - O O - O O - X O O O O O O O O O O - - X O O -
O O O - O O O - - - - - O - O - - - O - O O O O - O X - O O - O - - - O O - X O
O O O - - - - O - O O O O X - - O - - - O O X - - - - - O O O - X O - - O
O - O - - O - X - O X O - O O X O - - O O O X X O O O O - - - - - O - - O
O - - O O O - - - - O X O - O - - - - - - - O O - O - - O - O - - - X O - - - O
- O - - O - O O - - - O O O - - - O X O - O X X O O - O X - - O - O O O O - O O -
O O O O O - O - - O - O - O - O O O - - - O - O - - - O O O O X - O O O O -
- O - - O O X X O X - O X - O - - O - O - - O O X - O - O - O O O - O O O O O -
O O O O O O O X - O X - X O - O - - - O - O O X O O O X O X - O O O X X - - - X
X X O O O - - O O X - O O O - - - O X - - O O - O X X O - X O O X X O - - O O - - O
O O O O - O O X O X O O O - - - - O O O O O O O O O O O O - - - - - O - - - O O
O - X O - X O X - - O O O O - - O O X O - X X O O - - - - O - - X O - - O O O
```

```
X - X X X - X - X X X X X - X X X X - - X X X - X X - X X X X X X X - O - -
X X X - X - X - X X X X - X X - X X - - X X - X - X X X - X - X X X - X X - X X
X X X X X - X - - - - - O - - X X - X - X X - X - X - - X X X - X - - X - X X X
X X X - - O - X X X - - - X X X - X X X - X X X X X X X X X X X - - - - - O - X X
- X - X - - - X - X X X X X - X X X X - O - - - X X X X X - - X X X X - - - - - -
X X X X - X X X - - X X X - - - - X - X - X X X - X X - - O - X X - X X - O O O
X - X X X - - - X - X - - O - - X X - X X X - X X - X X - - X X X X X X X - - -
X X - X X - X X X X X X X - - - X X - X - - X - X - - X - X X X X X X - O O O
X X - - X - X X X - - X X - X X X X - X - - X X X X - X X - X - X X X - X X -
X - - - - X - - - - X X X X - X X X X - X X - X - X - X - X - X X X - - - - O O
- - X - X - X X X - - - X X - - X X X X X - - - X X X X X - X X X - - X X - X -
X - O - X X - - X X X - - X X - - X X - - X X X X - X X X X X X X - X X - - O
X - X X X X X - X - - X - - - - X X X X X - X X X X X X X X - - X - X -
X - X X - X - X X - X - - X X - X - - X - X - X X X - X X X - X X X - X - X X
X X - X X - X X - - - - X X - - X X - X - X - - X X - X - X X - - X X X X X X X
X X X - - X - X X - X X X X X X X X X - X X X - - - X X X - X - X - - X X X X X -
X X X - X X - - X - X X X X - X X X - X X X - - X - X X - X X X - X X - - X X
X X - X X X - X X - X X X X X X X - - X X X - X X X X X - X X X - X X X X X X -
- X - X X X X - X - - X X X - - - - X X - X X - X X X X X X X X X X X - - X X X -
X X X - X X X - - - - - X - X - - - X - X X X X - X X - X X - X - - - X X - X X
X X X - - - - X - X X X X X - - X - - - X X X - - - - - X X X - X X - - X
X - X - - X - X - X X X - X X X X - - X X X X X X X X X X - - - - - X - - X
X - - X X X - - - - X X X - X - - - - - - - X X - X - - X - X - - - X X - - - X
- X - - X - X X - - - X X X - - - X X X - X X X X X - X X - - X - X X X X - X X -
X X X X X - X - - X - X - X - X X X - - - X - X - - - X X X X X - X X X X -
- X - - X X X X O X - X X - X - - X - X - - X X X - X - X - X X X - X X X X X -
X X X X X X X X - X X - X X - X - - - X - X X X X X X X X X - X X X X X - - - X
X X X X X - - X X X - X X X - - - X X - - X X - X X X X - X X X X X X X - - X X - - X
X X X X - X X X X X X X X - - - - X X X X X X X X X X X X - - - - - X - - - X X
X - X X - X X X - - X X X X - - X X X X - X X X X - - - - X - - X X - - X X X
```

Code Listing 5.8: Connected components. Each social group is labeled

```
1 - 1 1 1 - 2 - 3 3 3 3 3 3 - - 4 4 4 4 - - 4 4 4 - 4 4 - 4 4 4 4 4 4 4 4 - 5 - -
1 1 1 - 1 - 2 - 3 3 3 3 - 3 3 - 4 4 - - 4 4 - 4 - 4 4 4 - 4 - 4 4 4 - 4 4 - 6 6
1 1 1 1 1 - 2 - - - - - 7 - - 4 4 - 4 - 4 4 - 4 - 4 - - 4 4 4 - 4 - - - 4 - 6 6 6
1 1 1 - - 8 - 4 4 4 - - - 4 4 4 - 4 4 4 - 4 4 4 4 4 4 4 4 4 4 4 - - - - - 9 - 6 6
- 1 - 1 - - 4 - 4 4 4 4 4 - 4 4 4 4 - A - - 4 4 4 4 4 - - 4 4 4 4 - 4 - - - - -
1 1 1 1 - 4 4 4 - - 4 4 4 - - - - 4 - 4 - 4 4 4 - 4 4 - - B - 4 4 - 4 4 - C C C
1 - 1 1 1 - - - 4 - 4 - - D - - 4 4 - 4 4 4 - 4 4 - 4 4 - - 4 4 4 4 4 4 4 - - -
1 1 - 1 1 - 4 4 4 4 4 4 4 - - - 4 4 - 4 - - E - 4 - - 4 - - 4 4 4 4 4 4 - F F F
1 1 - 1 - - 4 4 4 - - 4 4 - 4 4 4 4 - G - - 4 4 4 4 - 4 4 - 4 - 4 4 4 - F F -
1 - - - - H - - - - 4 4 4 4 4 - 4 4 4 4 - 4 4 - 4 - 4 - 4 - 4 4 4 - - - - F F
- - I - - H - J J J - - - 4 4 - - 4 4 4 4 4 - - - 4 4 4 4 4 - 4 4 4 - K K - F -
L - I - H H H - - - M M M - - N N - - 4 4 4 4 - - 4 - 4 4 - 4 4 4 4 - K K - - O
L - - H H H H - P - - M - - - - - - - 4 4 4 4 4 - 4 - 4 4 4 4 4 4 4 - - K - 4 -
L - H H - H - P P - Q - - R R - R - - - 4 - 4 - - 4 4 4 - 4 4 4 - 4 - - - 4 4
L L - H H - P P - - - - R R - - R R - 4 - 4 - - 4 4 - 4 - 4 4 - - 4 4 4 4 4 4 4
L L L - H - P P - R R R R R R R R R - 4 4 4 - - 4 4 4 - 4 - 4 - 4 4 4 4 4 4 4 -
L L L - H H - - - R R R R - R R R - 4 4 - 4 4 4 - 4 - 4 4 - 4 4 4 - 4 - - 4 4
L L - H H H - S S - R R R R R R R - 4 4 4 - 4 4 4 4 4 - 4 4 4 - 4 4 4 4 4 4 -
- L - H H H H - S - R R R - - - - T T - 4 4 - 4 4 4 4 4 4 4 4 4 4 - - 4 4 4 -
L L L - H H H - - - - - R - R - - - T - 4 4 4 4 - 4 4 - 4 4 - 4 - - - 4 4 - 4 4
L L L - - - - U - - R R R R R - V - - - - 4 4 4 - - - - - 4 4 4 - 4 - W - -
L - L - R - U - R R R - R R R R - 4 4 4 4 4 4 4 4 4 - - 4 - - - - X - - Y
L - - R R R - - - - R R R - R - - - - - - 4 4 - 4 - - 4 - 4 - - - 4 4 - - - Y
- R - - R - R R - - R R R - - Z - a a - 4 4 4 4 - 4 4 - - 4 - 4 4 4 4 - 4 4 -
R R R R R - - - R - R - b - a a a - - 4 - 4 - - 4 4 4 4 - 4 - 4 4 - 4 4 -
- R - - R R R R R - R R - b - - a - 4 4 4 - 4 - 4 - 4 4 4 - 4 4 4 4 4 4 4
R R R R R R R - R R - R R - c - - - 4 - 4 4 4 4 4 4 4 4 - 4 4 4 4 4 - - - 4
R R R R - R R R - R R R - c c - - 4 4 - 4 4 4 4 - 4 4 4 4 4 4 - - 4 4 - - - 4
R R R R - R R R R R R R - - - - 4 4 4 4 4 4 4 4 4 4 4 4 4 - - - - - 4 - - - 4 4
R - R R - R R R - - R R R R R - - 4 4 4 4 - 4 4 4 4 - - - - d - - 4 4 - - 4 4 4
```

Lab514: Connected Components

One reason to model the spread of disease so quickly is *contingency planning*.

Rather than marking non-empty slots as sick or healthy mark them now as merely being occupied. Then, label each social circle by assigning a group number to those slots that are connected (directly or indirectly) together. Of course each different social circle will need a different group number. Algorithm 5.1.1 outlines your code and Code Listing 5.8 shows the desired output for our favorite 2-D grid.

Algorithm 5.1.1 A function $label(grid)$ that labels the connected components

---

1: $group = 1$
2: **while** $j = 0, 1, 2, \ldots$ **do**
3:    **if** *unnumbered* **then**
4:       $grid[j] = group$
5:       *floodfill*
6:       $group = group + 1$
7:    **end if**
8: **end while**

Code Listing 5.9: Is there a component that spans the grid? Yes or no?

```
- - 1 - - 2 - 2 2 2 2 - - 3 - 3 - 3 3 3 3 - 4 4 - 5 5 - - - 6 6 - 7 7 7 - - - 8
3 - 1 - 2 2 - - - - 2 - 3 3 3 3 - - 3 - - 9 - - 5 5 5 5 5 5 - - 7 7 7 - - - A -
3 - - 2 2 2 2 - 2 2 2 - 3 3 - 3 - - 3 3 - 9 9 - 5 5 - - 5 - 7 7 7 7 7 - - - A A
3 - - - 2 - 2 2 2 2 - B - 3 - 3 3 3 3 3 3 - 9 9 - - 5 5 5 5 - 7 7 - - A A - A A
3 3 3 3 - C - 2 2 2 2 - - 3 3 - - - - - 3 3 - - - 5 5 - - 5 - - - D - A A A A -
3 3 - - 3 - - - - 2 - - 3 - - 3 3 - 3 - 3 - - - E - - 3 - 5 5 5 - - A A A A A A
- 3 3 3 3 3 - F - - 3 3 3 - 3 - 3 3 3 3 3 3 - 3 - - 3 3 - - 5 - - - G - - - - A A
- - 3 3 3 - H - 3 3 3 3 3 - 3 3 3 - - 3 - - 3 3 3 3 3 3 - I - - J - - A - A A A
3 3 3 3 3 3 - 3 3 3 3 3 3 3 3 3 3 3 - - 3 3 3 - 3 - 3 3 3 - - - - K - A A A A -
- - 3 - 3 3 3 3 3 - 3 3 3 - - 3 - 3 - 3 3 - - - - - 3 3 - - L - K K K - - A A -
3 3 - M - - 3 3 3 - 3 3 3 3 3 3 3 - 3 3 3 3 3 3 3 3 3 3 3 3 - - - K K - - - A A A
- 3 3 - N - - 3 3 - - 3 3 3 3 3 3 3 - 3 3 - 3 3 3 - - 3 3 - - - - - O - - A A A
- 3 3 - N - 3 3 3 3 - 3 3 - 3 - - 3 - - 3 3 3 3 3 3 - 3 3 - 3 3 3 - 3 - 3 - A - -
3 3 3 3 - - 3 3 - - 3 3 3 3 3 - - 3 3 3 3 3 3 3 3 3 3 3 3 3 - 3 3 3 3 - A A A
3 3 3 - 3 3 3 - 3 3 3 3 3 3 - 3 3 - - - 3 - - 3 - - 3 - - 3 - 3 3 3 3 3 - - - P - - -
- - 3 3 3 - - - 3 - 3 3 - - 3 3 - 3 3 - 3 3 - - - 3 - - 3 3 3 - 3 3 - - - 3 3 3
- 3 3 - 3 - - 3 3 - - 3 - 3 3 3 3 3 3 3 3 - 3 3 3 3 - - 3 3 3 3 - 3 3 3 3 3 - - -
- 3 - Q - - 3 3 - - 3 3 3 3 3 3 3 3 3 3 - 3 3 3 - - 3 3 - 3 3 - 3 3 - 3 3 3 3 - 3 3 3
- - R - - 3 3 3 3 - - - 3 - - 3 3 - 3 3 - 3 3 - 3 3 3 - - - - - - - 3 3 - - 3 3 -
R R R - 3 3 - 3 3 3 - 3 3 3 - S - - T - - - 3 3 3 3 - - 3 3 - 3 3 - U - 3 3 3 3 - 3 3 -
- R R - - 3 3 - 3 - - - 3 3 - 3 3 3 - 3 3 3 3 - 3 - - 3 3 3 - - - 3 3 3 3 3 - 3 3
R R R R - - - 3 3 - 3 3 3 - 3 3 3 - - 3 3 - 3 - - - V - - 3 3 3 3 - - - W - 3
R R - - - - - 3 3 3 3 3 3 - 3 3 - 3 3 3 3 3 - 3 3 - X - - - - - 3 3 - 3 - - - -
R R R - Y Y Y - 3 3 3 - - - - 3 - 3 3 - 3 3 3 - 3 3 - X - - - Z - 3 3 3 3 3 - 3
R - - Y Y - Y - - - 3 3 - - a - 3 3 3 - 3 - 3 - - - 3 - - - Z Z Z Z - - 3 3 3 3 3
R - Y Y - - - - 3 3 3 - - a - 3 3 - 3 3 - 3 3 3 3 3 3 3 - - Z - Z Z - 3 3 - - 3
R - Y - - Y Y - - - 3 - b - c - 3 3 3 - 3 3 3 - - 3 - 3 - - - Z Z - 3 3 - d - -
- Y Y Y Y Y Y - e - 3 - - - - - 3 - - 3 3 3 3 3 - - 3 3 3 - - - Z - - - - - - f
g - - Y Y Y Y - e - 3 - h h - 3 3 3 - - - - 3 - - i - - - - i - - j j - k - 1 -
g g - Y Y Y Y - - 3 3 3 - h - 3 - - - 3 3 3 3 3 - i i i i i i - - - j - - 1 1 1
```

Lab515: Spanning

Does any group reach all four borders of the grid?

We want to answer this single question, yes or no, and if yes then we also report the group number. Such a component is said to "span" the grid. Code Listing 5.9 shows a case where there is a spanning component, thus the answer is Yes, component 3 spans the grid. On the previous page the answer was No, there is no spanning component for this grid. (Closest was #4 shown in bold.) Assuming the groups are already labeled then Algorithm 5.1.2 outlines a function to check for spanning.

Algorithm 5.1.2 A function $span(grid)$ that checks for a spanning component

---

1: **while** $group = 1, 2, 3, \ldots$ **do**
2:   **if** $span(group)$ **then**
3:     **return true**
4:   **end if**
5: **end while**
6: **return false**

Fig. 5.2: Runtime analysis, recursion versus a loop and a list.

5.2 Runtime Analysis

A certain problem of size $n = 31$ has a runtime of 0.75 seconds. Increasing the size
to $n = 33$ then takes almost 2 seconds, and for $n = 37$ over 13 seconds. Why?

It gets worse. If the trend continues then $n = 51$ will take over 10,000 seconds or
almost three hours. Likewise, $n = 65$ needs nearly 10,000,000 seconds or 15 weeks.
Ridiculously, $n = 75$ runs for over 1,000,000,000 seconds, just shy of 36 years.

Lab521: Fibonacci Numbers

The scenario described above is based on exponential growth. Figures 5.2 and 5.3
indicate a similar runtime for the Fibonacci function shown in Code Listing 5.10.

Note the dramatic changes in vertical scale between the two plots whereas the
problem size has not moved that far along the horizontal axis. If recursion is desired
then Code Listing 5.11 suggests an incremental (inchworming) treatment of

$$F_n = F_{n-1} + F_{n-2}$$

and $F_1 = F_2 = 1$, a tail recursion that translates into code using just a loop and a list.

Code Listing 5.10: The "classic" recursive implementation

```
#
def F(n):
    if n==1 or n==2:
        return 1
    else:
        return F(n-1)+F(n-2)  # two recursive calls
#
```

Code Listing 5.11: Tail recursion and a form of "inchworming"

```
#
def F(n,k,next,prev):
    if n==k:
        return prev
    else:
        return F(n,k+1,next+prev,next)
#
fibn=F(n,1,1,1)  # base case specified when called
#
```

Fig. 5.3: Runtime analysis, recursion versus a loop and a list, continued

Lab522: Euclid's Algorithm

This famous algorithm for calculating the greatest common divisor (GCD) of two positive integers (a and b) comes from Euclid's *The Elements*, circa 500 B.C.

See Code Listing 5.12 for the procedure and Table 5.1 for an example. We could also use a loop instead of recursion but either way Euclid's approach offers a clear improvement over other standard methods:

1. Loop from 1 up to $min(a,b)$ remembering only the last common divisor you see. Since the loop goes up, when it finishes the last one you saw must be the greatest.
2. Loop from $min(a,b)$ down to 1 stopping as soon as you find a common divisor. If you make it all the way down to 1 then a and b are said to be *relatively prime*.

Code Listing 5.12: Tail recursion again, which could be coded with just a loop

```
#
def gcd(a,b):
    #
    mod=(a%b)
    #
    if mod==0:
        return b
    else:
        return gcd(b,mod)
    #
#
```

Table 5.1: Trace of an example GCD calculation using Euclid's algorithm

Call	a	b	mod
1	20	72	20
2	72	20	12
3	20	12	8
4	12	8	4
5	8	4	0

Code Listing 5.13 shows three more test cases, but of course you can come up with a set of your own cases, too. Note how in the last case Euclid requires only a single step, and not $O(1000)$, to determine that 999 and 1000 are relatively prime.

Code Listing 5.13: A small set of test cases

```
  20   72:  4
 230 4050:  10
 999 1000:  1
```

System Call Stack

What does the computer actually do when we make a recursive call? Say we are in the main program and we call $gcd(70, 15)\ldots$

$$(main) \rightarrow gcd(70, 15)$$
$$gcd(70, 15) \rightarrow gcd(15, 10)$$
$$gcd(15, 10) \rightarrow gcd(10, 5)$$
$$gcd(10, 5) \rightarrow STOP$$

But when the last recursive call returns "the answer" it does so only to the previous recursive call, who must pass it on, who must pass it on...

$$gcd(10, 5) \rightarrow 5 \rightarrow gcd(15, 10)$$
$$gcd(15, 10) \rightarrow 5 \rightarrow gcd(70, 15)$$
$$gcd(70, 15) \rightarrow 5 \rightarrow (main)$$

In this way the answer (5) is finally returned to the original call of $gcd(70, 15)$ in our main program. Table 5.2 shows the system call stack during execution of this recursive function, assuming that successive calls occupy contiguous memory.

Table 5.2: Diagram of system call stack

	⋮	
call #1	argument #2	$b = 15$
	argument #1	$a = 70$
	return address	main program
	local variable	$mod = 10$
call #2	argument #2	$b = 10$
	argument #1	$a = 15$
	return address	call #1
	local variable	$mod = 5$
call #3	argument #2	$b = 5$
	argument #1	$a = 10$
	return address	call #2
	local variable	$mod = 0$
	⋮	

Now you can see why there has to be a recursive depth limit. Each function call accounts for a non-zero amount of *memory* and there is finite memory available to any computer. This also suggests that we could code "recursion" using only an explicit stack and (!) no function.

Fill-the-Area Tool

A stack may be used for a fill-the-area tool mentioned in Lab235 and Lab513.

Figure 5.4 on the next page shows two 400×300 images. The top image was produced interactively with Code Listing 5.14 below, combining ideas from Lab131, Lab214, and Lab233. Since there are 120,000 pixels total, filling-the-area for the bottom image could require a large number of putpixel calls.

If each of these calls is made within a recursive floodfill function then we will often exceed the depth limit. Alternatively, the approach outlined in Algorithm 5.2.1 performs the same putpixel calls but with an explicit stack instead.

Code Listing 5.14: A combination of Lab131, Lab214, and Lab233

```
#
def drag(evnt):
    global x,y,pmg
    #
    t=0.0
    while t<=1.0:
        xp=int(x+t*(evnt.x-x)+0.5)
        yp=int(y+t*(evnt.y-y)+0.5)
        img.putpixel((xp,yp),(0,0,0))
        #
        t+=0.001
    #
    pmg=ImageTk.PhotoImage(img)
    cnvs.itemconfigure(tkid,image=pmg)
    #
    x=evnt.x
    y=evnt.y
#
```

Algorithm 5.2.1 Filling-the-area with a stack. Initial xy determined interactively

---

 1: $push(xy)$
 2: **while** *nonempty* **do**
 3:       $xy = pop()$
 4:       $putpixel(xy, gray)$
 5:       **while** $nxy = nbr(xy)$ **do**
 6:            **if** $check(nxy)$ **then**
 7:                 $push(nxy)$
 8:            **end if**
 9:       **end while**
10: **end while**

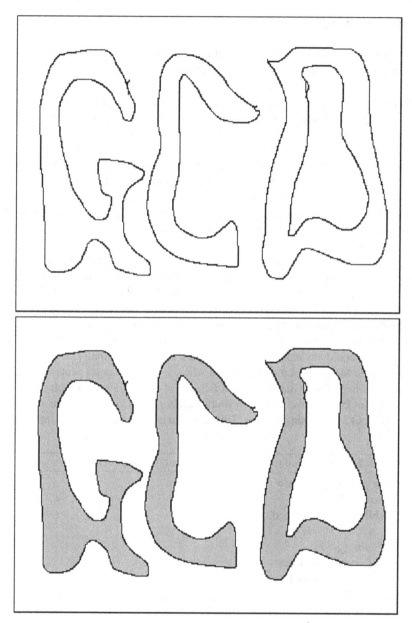

Fig. 5.4: Fill-the-Area Tool. *Top*: The letters G-C-D, before. *Bottom*: After three separate operations where 11,674 total `putpixel` calls were used to fill the 'G', 8,555 calls for 'C', and 13,759 for 'D'. Each letter made $O(10\%)$ of the pixels gray but if we filled *outside* the letters then most of the pixels would change all at once

Lab523: Spanning Plot

Your assignment is to produce the first plot shown in Fig. 5.5, the top one.

Using our previous code to determine whether or not there is a connected component that spans a grid, Algorithm 5.2.2 loops p from 0.0 to 1.0 and finds for each different p the likelihood that a spanning component will exist. So, the horizontal axis in our plot shows the value of p and the vertical axis shows what fraction of the associated trials had a spanning component present for that p.

These plots both used 1000 trials. Running more trials would make the plot smoother, as would incrementing p more finely (as shown $dp = 0.01$), however both of those refinements will have an associated runtime cost.

Note carefully in the algorithm how p only determines initialization of the grid. From the plots we see that for $p < 0.5$ there is "never" a spanning component and for $p > 0.7$ there "always" is one. For the in-between range we transition toward ever more likely spanning as p increases.

As we scale the size of our grid toward infinity (an order of magnitude increase is shown in the bottom plot) this transition will sharpen until eventually we see only a step-function that jumps directly from 0% to 100% at the *critical probability*.

To save on runtime in both zooming and sharpening it is only necessary to refine our plot locally near this critical probability. We certainly never need to do any refinement where we already know the spanning percentage is either 0% or 100% because how could any change possibly make a difference to that!?

Unlike the Mandelbrot movie problem where a small program generated a large amount of image-frame data in a short amount of time, drawing a high-resolution spanning plot involves the input of a single value, p, then your code runs for hours, only to output another single value. This scenario is ideal for parallel computing.

Algorithm 5.2.2 Observed probability of a spanning component

 1: **while** $p = 0.0 \rightarrow 1.0$ **do**
 2:    $count = 0$
 3:    **while** $t = 1 \rightarrow trials$ **do**
 4:       $initialize(grid, p)$
 5:       $label(grid)$
 6:       **if** $span(grid)$ **then**
 7:          $count = count + 1$
 8:       **end if**
 9:    **end while**
10:    **print** $p, count/trials$
11: **end while**

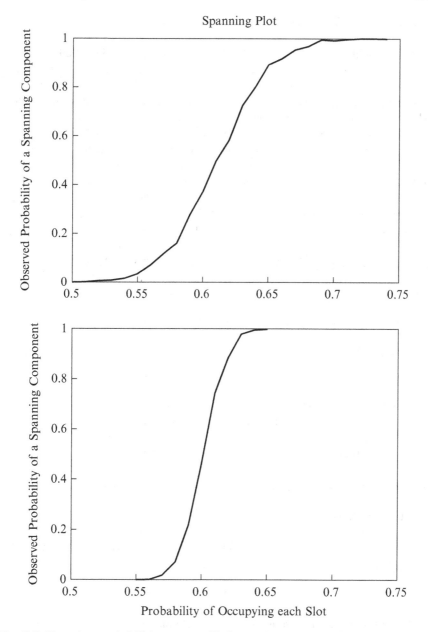

Fig. 5.5: For what probabilities are we likely to observe a spanning component? *Top*: grid size 40×30. *Bottom*: grid size 120×90, an order of magnitude larger

Lab524: Forest Fire

The next few pages show the simulation of a forest fire ignited on the left edge of
our grid that moves through populated slots and eventually burns out. We want to
know how the average burnout time changes as the density of trees is varied.

Our floodfill algorithm would recursively burn up the entire forest in one step,
which is not an accurate representation of a fire. We need to advance step-by-step
so we can count the number of steps it takes for the fire to burn out.

Code Listing 5.15 advances the fire a single step where currently burning trees
ignite their nearest neighbors and then burn out themselves. In the grid plots shown
in Code Listings 5.16, 5.17, and 5.18, the asterisks ($*$) from the code appear as
filled-in black dots. Note how the code uses 'F' to mark trees as "going to be on
fire" but we never see this character in any of the plots.

Your code should also calculate burnout time and display a running step count.

Code Listing 5.15: Forest fire, advancing step-by-step to nearest neighbors

```
#
j=0
while j<w*h:
    if grid[j]=='*':
        #
        y=j/w
        x=j%w
        #
        maybe_ignite(grid,x,y-1) # up
        maybe_ignite(grid,x,y+1) # down
        maybe_ignite(grid,x-1,y) # left
        maybe_ignite(grid,x+1,y) # right
    j+=1
#
j=0
while j<w*h:
    if grid[j]=='*': grid[j]=' ' # burning --> out
    if grid[j]=='F': grid[j]='*' # ignited --> burn
    j+=1
#
```

A fast running alternative is to use a special kind of list called a *queue*, similar
to a system call stack only where items are added and removed from different ends
of the list. The advancing-front characteristic of the forest fire is related to a famous
technique known as *breadth-first search*. Again, since there is a time component to
our fire burning out it does not make sense to recursively floodfill all the way across
the forest at once. We could modify Lab513 in the same way.

Code Listing 5.16: Forest fire. Top: Initial conditions. Bottom: After five steps

Code Listing 5.17: Forest fire. Top: After 10 steps. Bottom: After 20 steps

Code Listing 5.18: Forest fire. Top: After 40 steps. Bottom: Done after 78 steps

Fig. 5.6: Burnout time, on average, as the density of trees is varied

Lab525: Burnout Time

Your assignment is to generate a plot similar to the one shown in Fig. 5.6 which used 1000 trials for each different density of trees.

In the bottom-left we see that very sparse forests burn out quickly because the fire has nowhere to spread.

To the right-hand side we see that very dense forests have a burnout time proportional to the width (here the grid was 40×30) because the fire spreads directly across the forest without having to make its way back-and-forth at all.

Closer to the familiar looking critical probability we might expect a spanning component of the grid to just barely reach all four borders. In this case the fire takes a long time to travel up and down and left and right through all the fractal-like tendrils of the forest.

As we scale the size of the grid toward infinity the peak burnout time itself goes to infinity and forms a vertical asymptote at the critical probability. Wow!

Plots for different grid sizes are shown in Fig. 5.7 where the vertical scale has been adjusted for comparison; alternatively, we might *normalize* the burnout time by dividing it by the width of the grid.

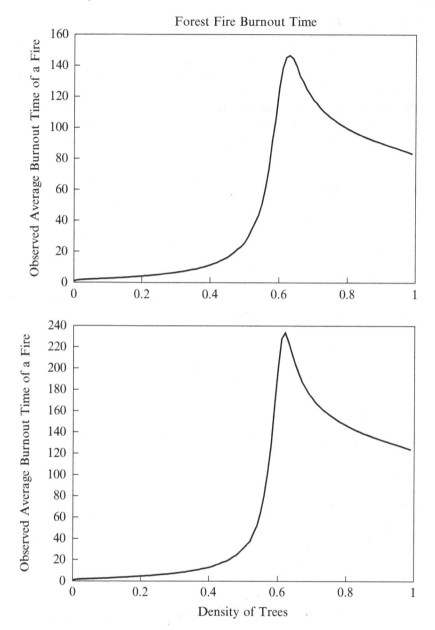

Fig. 5.7: Burnout time, continued. *Top*: Grid is 80×60. *Bottom*: Grid is 120×90. A larger grid represents a more fine-grain resolution and not a larger overall forest

5.3 Guessing Games

Consider two games, first a simple case of flipping a coin and guessing heads or tails
and then a more complicated game where we guess higher or lower as a sequence
of the digits 1–9 is constructed.

The coin-flipping game is presented for the sake of comparison because it is so
much easier to analyze than high-low. In particular, for coin flips there is only one
successful path through the game: always guess the next 50-50 flip correctly.

Lab531: Independent Events

We try to guess if a coin will land on heads or tails when flipped and we assume
there is no cheating so the chance of success is really 50%. It does not matter if we
guess heads, guess tails, or guess at random; all three "strategies" have the same
success rate and if we run $10,000$ trials the odds will average out close enough.

So, how likely are we to end the game having guessed n flips correctly in a row?
The answer is $1/2^{n+1}$ where the "plus one" accounts for the fact that we must guess
the last coin flip wrong to end the streak, also a 50-50 chance.

Figure 5.8 confirms this but you should write your own code to convince yourself.

Fig. 5.8: Guessing coin flips. Before we flip the first coin a streak of nine steps is
highly unlikely: less than one-tenth of one percent. But if we have already guessed
eight flips correctly then the chance of a ninth is 50-50, a coin flip

Fig. 5.9: Guessing high or low. Before we make the first guess a streak of nine steps has a 1.3 % chance of occurring. So, we have a better chance here than we did just flipping coins but surviving the first guess is still 50-50, a "coin flip"

Lab532: High or Low

In the high-low game we start always with the number 5 first. The next number cannot be the same as the current number so the second number will never be 5.

Numbers are chosen from the digits 1–9 and you guess if the next number will be higher or lower than the current one. Many paths are possible. If you guess lower on the first turn then it could be a 1 or a 2 or a 3 or a 4. In the sample runs shown in both Code Listings 5.19 and 5.20 the "lower" and "higher" were typed by the user.

Code Listing 5.19: A sample run with a four-guess winning streak

```
Number is 5.   Next will be... high or low?   lower
Number is 2.   Next will be... high or low?   higher
Number is 9.   Next will be... high or low?   lower
Number is 7.   Next will be... high or low?   lower
Number is 5.   Next will be... high or low?   lower

Number is 7.   Game over.   Correct guesses:   4
```

Code Listing 5.20: Sample runs with a variety of streaks

```
Number is 5.  Next will be... high or low?  lower
Number is 2.  Next will be... high or low?  higher
Number is 3.  Next will be... high or low?  higher
Number is 4.  Next will be... high or low?  higher
Number is 6.  Next will be... high or low?  lower
Number is 1.  Next will be... high or low?  higher
Number is 6.  Next will be... high or low?  lower
Number is 3.  Next will be... high or low?  higher
Number is 2.  Game over.  Correct guesses:  7

Number is 5.  Next will be... high or low?  lower
Number is 2.  Next will be... high or low?  higher
Number is 6.  Next will be... high or low?  lower
Number is 3.  Next will be... high or low?  higher
Number is 8.  Next will be... high or low?  lower
Number is 6.  Next will be... high or low?  lower
Number is 3.  Next will be... high or low?  higher
Number is 9.  Next will be... high or low?  lower
Number is 1.  Next will be... high or low?  higher
Number is 3.  Next will be... high or low?  higher
Number is 8.  Next will be... high or low?  lower
Number is 7.  Next will be... high or low?  lower
Number is 6.  Next will be... high or low?  lower
Number is 8.  Game over.  Correct guesses:  12

Number is 5.  Next will be... high or low?  lower
Number is 1.  Next will be... high or low?  higher
Number is 7.  Next will be... high or low?  lower
Number is 9.  Game over.  Correct guesses:  2

Number is 5.  Next will be... high or low?  lower
Number is 6.  Game over.  Correct guesses:  0

Number is 5.  Next will be... high or low?  lower
Number is 4.  Next will be... high or low?  higher
Number is 1.  Game over.  Correct guesses:  1

Number is 5.  Next will be... high or low?  lower
Number is 8.  Game over.  Correct guesses:  0

Number is 5.  Next will be... high or low?  lower
Number is 9.  Game over.  Correct guesses:  0
```

Lab533: Optimal Play

Algorithm 5.3.1 outlines an optimal strategy and Fig. 5.9 previously showed our expected results. Algorithm 5.3.2 outlines the structure of an overall simulation which could also implement coin-flipping if we substitute a different call for *game*.

Algorithm 5.3.1 A function *game*() that plays high-low with an optimal strategy

---
1: *streak* = 0
2: *number* = 5
3: **while true do**
4:     **if** *number* < 5 **then**
5:         *guess* = *higher*
6:     **else if** *number* > 5 **then**
7:         *guess* = *lower*
8:     **else**
9:         *guess* = *random*
10:     **end if**
11:     *nextnumber* = *generate*
12:     **if** *correct* **then**
13:         *streak* = *streak* + 1
14:         *number* = *nextnumber*
15:     **else**
16:         **return** *streak*
17:     **end if**
18: **end while**

Algorithm 5.3.2 A simulation to determine the likelihood of various streaks

---
1: *count* = *hashtable*
2: **while** *t* = 1 → *trials* **do**
3:     *streak* = *game*()
4:     **if** *first* **then**
5:         *count*[*streak*] = 1
6:     **else**
7:         *count*[*streak*] = *count*[*streak*] + 1
8:     **end if**
9: **end while**
10: **while** *streak* = 0 → *max*(*streak*) **do**
11:     **if** *nonzero* **then**
12:         **print** *streak*, *count*[*streak*]/*trials*
13:     **end if**
14: **end while**

Lab534: All Possible Games

An alternative to randomized simulation (which may play out the same exact game multiple times) is to use recursion and generate all possible game paths directly.

This is straightforward with heads-tails because we can list out possible games using the binary representation of integers, 0=heads and 1=tails. There are 2^n different bitstrings with length n where we "pad" the front as in 00110001.

Code Listing 5.21 shows a similar, albeit more meandering, enumeration of all possible paths for high-low. This recursive function is called using: `recur([5])`

Code Listing 5.21: Recursively print all possible high-low game paths

```
def recur(seqnums):
    #
    if len(seqnums)>maxstreak:
        print seqnums+['...']
        return
    #
    num=seqnums[-1]        # current number
    #
    # loop over all possible next numbers
    #
    nextnum=1
    while nextnum<=9:
        #
        if num==nextnum:  # prohibited
            pass
        #
        elif num<5 and nextnum<num:
            print seqnums+[nextnum,'lose']
        elif num>5 and nextnum>num:
            print seqnums+[nextnum,'lose']
        #
        # assume we guess 'lower' on a 5
        #
        elif num==5 and nextnum>num:
            print seqnums+[nextnum,'lose']
        #
        # finally now, a correct guess...
        #
        else:
            recur(seqnums+[nextnum])
        #
        nextnum+=1
    #
#
```

Lab535: Analytic Calculation

Using the tree of all possible paths we can also calculate the likelihood of any particular length streak. In fact, previously mentioned Fig. 5.9 shows simulation results overlaid with precisely these analytic findings.

Code Listing 5.22 shows our recursive function where the argument p indicates the probability that we have even made it this far and p diminishes by a factor of eight down each particular path. To start use: `calc(0,5,1.0)`

Note that simulation runtime for similarly accurate results may be much faster.

Code Listing 5.22: Recursively calculate the probability of each game path

```
htable={}
#
def calc(streak,num,p):
    #
    if streak>maxstreak:
        return
    #
    # How likely is the streak to end now?
    #
    chances=4+abs(5-num)
    if streak not in htable:
        htable[streak]=0.0
    htable[streak]+=(p*(1.0-chances/8.0))
    #
    if num>=5:
        #
        # in this case we guess lower...
        #
        nextnum=1
        while nextnum<num:
            calc(streak+1,nextnum,p/8.0)
            nextnum+=1
        #
    else:
        #
        # in this case we guess higher...
        #
        nextnum=num+1
        while nextnum<=9:
            calc(streak+1,nextnum,p/8.0)
            nextnum+=1
        #
    #
#
```

Recursive Tree

Figure 5.10 shows the beginning of our random tree from Lab225, when 800 turtles were used to draw *almost* an entire tree.

Code Listing 5.23 shows an alternative approach using recursion. Now only a single turtle is used, with no randomness, and it draws the entire tree all by itself, actually twice: once walking forward and then again walking backward.

In this case it is important that the left and right angles balance each other precisely or else our turtle would drift off-course. Also, any colors used in the drawing must be set when walking backward because that part happens last.

Code Listing 5.23: A tree being drawn recursively by a single turtle

```
. . .
#
def tree(n):
    #
    if n<=0.0: return # base case
    #
    move(n)                # forward
    #
    turn( 28.0)            # left
    tree(n-5.0)            # recursion
    turn(-28.0)
    #
    turn(-28.0)            # right
    tree(n-5.0)            # recursion
    turn( 28.0)
    #
    move(-n)               # backward
#
################################################
#
img=Image.new('RGB',(320,240),(210,180,140))
#
xt=160.0
yt=225.0
ht=90.0
#
tree(45.0) # size of trunk ... not an angle
#
img.save('tree.png')
#
```

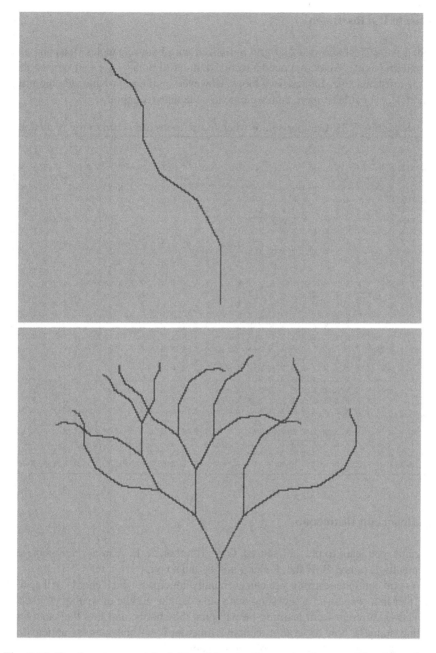

Fig. 5.10: Random tree, revisited. *Top*: After the first turtle. *Bottom*: After 10 turtles. In the end 800 turtles walked almost all of the $2^9 - 1 = 511$ branches of the tree.

When to Use Recursion

Code Listing 5.24 shows a 2-D grid initialized with both rectangles (left) and also at random (right). We do not need a recursive floodfill to label the four connections on the left-hand side. Just use two loops. However, on the right-hand side loops are insufficient, or at least more cumbersome to code than recursion.

Code Listing 5.24: Comparison of when to use loops and when to use recursion

```
- - - - - - - - - - - - - - - - - - - - - - X X X - X X - X X X X X X X - X - -
- X X X X - - - - - - - - - - - - - - - - - X - X - X X X - X - X X X - X X - X X
- X X X X - - - - - - - - - - - - - - - - - X - X - X - - X X X - X - - X - X X X
- X X X X - - - - - - - - - - - - - - - - - X X X X X X X X X X - - - - - X - X X
- X X X X - - - X X X X X X X X X X - - - - - X X X X X - - X X X X - X - - - - -
- X X X X - - - X X X X X X X X X X - - - X X X - X X - - X - X X - X X - X X - X X X
- X X X X - - - X X X X X X X X X X - - - X - X X - X X - - X X X X X X X - - -
- X X X X - - - X X X X X X X X X X - - - - X - X - - X - - X X X X X X - X X X
- X X X X - - - X X X X X X X X X X - - - - - X X X X - X X - X - X X X - X X -
- X X X X - - - X X X X X X X X X X - - - X X - X - X - X - X - X X X - - - - X X
- X X X X - - - - - - - - - - - - - - - - - X - - X X X X X - X X X - X X - X -
- X X X X - - - - - - - - - - - - - - - - X X - - X - X X - X X X - X X - - X
- X X X X - X X X X X X X X X X X X X X - - X X X - X - X X X X X X X - - X - X -
- X X X X - X X X X X X X X X X X X X X - - X - X X X - X X X - X X X - X - - X X
- X X X X - X X X X X X X X X X X X X X - - X - - - X X - X - X X - - X X X X X X X
- - - - - - X X X X X X X X X X X X X X - - X - - X X X - X - X - X X X X X X X
- - - - - - X X X X X X X X X X X X X X - - X X X - X - X X - - X X X - X - - X X
- - - - - - X X X X X X X X X X X X X X - - X - X X X X X - X X X - X X X X X X -
- - - - - - X X X X X X X X X X X X X X - - X - X X X X X X X X X X X - - X X X -
- - - - - - X X X X X X X X X X X X X X - - - X X X - - - - - X X X - X - X - -
- - - - - - X X X X X X X X X X X X X X - - X X X X X X X X - - X - - - - X - - X
- - - - - - X X X X X X X X X X X X X X - - - X X - X - - X - X - - - X X - - - X
- - - - - - X X X X X X X X X X X X X X - - - X X X X - X X - - X - X X X X - X X -
- - - - - - X X X X X X X X X X X X X X - - - X - X - - X X X X - X - X X - X X -
- - - - - - - - - - - - - - - - - - - - - - X X - - X - X - X X X - X X X X X X X
X X X X X X X X X X X X X X X X X - - - - - X X X X X X X X X - X X X X X - - - X
X X X X X X X X X X X X X X X X X - - - - - X X X - X X X X X X - - X X - - - - X
X X X X X X X X X X X X X X X X X - - - - - X X X X X X X X - - - - - X - - - X X
X X X X X X X X X X X X X X X X X - - - - - - X X X - - - - X - - X X - - X X X
```

An Important Distinction

In guitar you learn to play a D-chord, G, C, E minor, A, E, A minor, D minor, and eventually B minor, B, B-flat, F-sharp minor, and so on.

As you continue learning you can eventually anticipate which chords will appear together in a song, even a new song that you are in the middle of writing yourself.

This is different from learning how to play the chords, and it is the same with coding: namely, how to write a recursive function is not the same as anticipating when recursion might help you solve a problem.

Chapter 6
Projects

Everyone has ideas, and part of the joy of computing is to see your ideas come alive.

Three very different types of projects are presented in this chapter with the hope that everyone will find something that speaks to them. A few guidelines:

- Build everything up step-by-step... test as you go!
- Think about the big picture even as you struggle with the small details.
- Watch out for feature-creep. Keep in mind, what are you trying to do?

6.1 Sliding Tile Puzzle

Imagine a 4×4 grid of tiles where one tile has been removed. There are always at least two tiles next to the blank space and any tile next to the blank can slide over, effectively swapping positions. Tiles move horizontally and vertically but only in discrete chunks; it would not make any sense to slide a tile halfway into a slot.

Starting small, we begin with just text where Code Listing 6.1 shows how to create a generic text object at screen coordinates (xp, yp) displaying an empty string in a large font, and then also how to modify its text at a later time.

The illusion of the tiles is maintained by a rectangular grid drawn only in the background that does not move. Arrange these however you like but also plan ahead, we may scale the size to as much as 10×10 so write your code for an $n \times n$ grid.

Code Listing 6.1: Creating a Tk text object and remembering its ID number

```
#
f=('Times',36,'bold')
#
tkid=cnvs.create_text(xp,yp,text='',font=f)
#
cnvs.itemconfigure(tkid,text='Tile #1')
#
```

© Springer International Publishing 2016

S. Torbert, *Applied Computer Science*, DOI 10.1007/978-3-319-30866-1_6

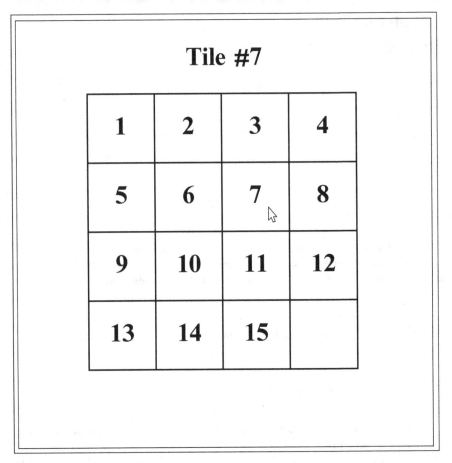

Fig. 6.1: Click tile, the text at top updates the tile number as the user clicks

Lab611: Click Tile

We may determine which tile is clicked, if any, by translating from pixel coordinates evnt.x and evnt.y into column and row (x,y) coordinates in the 4×4 puzzle. Here x and y are each 0, 1, 2, or 3. From these 2-D values the 1-D index is found directly using $4y + x$ because each row contains four slots. As shown in Fig. 6.1 we might display "BLANK" if the blank space is clicked or "You missed!" if the user happens to click somewhere completely outside the puzzle region.

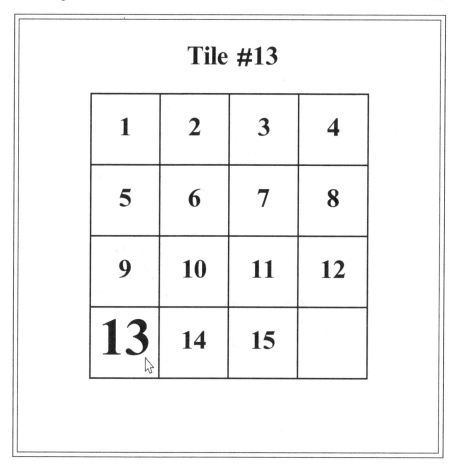

Fig. 6.2: Change tile, the text at top is still updated as before and now the tile's text object is also modified to show where the user has clicked

Lab612: Change Tile

In order to change the font of a particular tile's text object, as shown in Fig. 6.2, we must store all their Tk ID numbers in a list. There are two obvious ways to reset the previous tile's font back to normal: (1) set the font of all tiles after every click; and (2) remember which tile was clicked last and only reset it. Since n^2 is small in this case, either approach runs fast enough that the user cannot tell the difference.

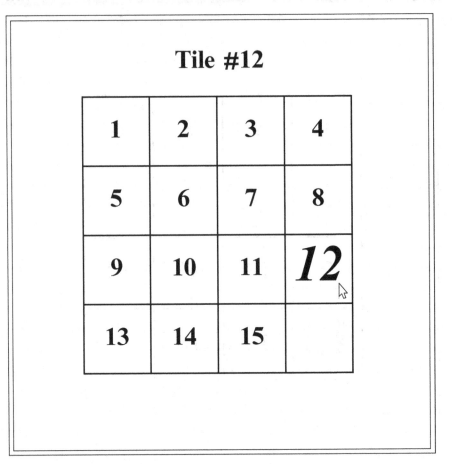

Fig. 6.3: Neighbor of blank, while the other tiles continue to be modified as before, the neighbors of the blank space are now treated differently when clicked

Lab613: Neighbor of Blank

We may italicize a font using:

```
f=('Times',72,'bold italic')
```

and Fig. 6.3 shows how this might then indicate a clicked tile differently if it also happens to be a neighbor of the blank space.

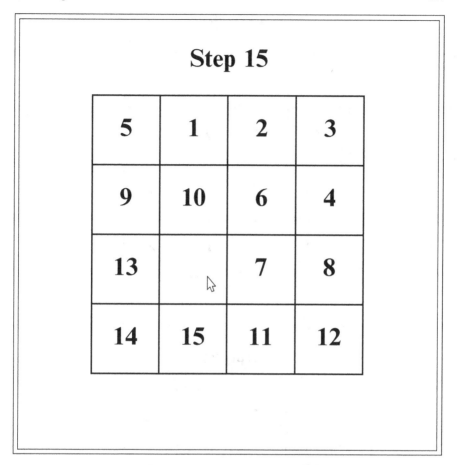

Fig. 6.4: Slide tile, where quite obviously the user has clicked the tiles in a spiral pattern and thus the "puzzle" is not much of a challenge

Lab614: Slide Tile

Now we want the tiles to move. At first the tile number corresponds to our list index but after a sequence of moves it may not. We can find the current text using:

```
num=cnvs.itemcget(tiles[j],'text')
```

Figures 6.4 and 6.5–6.6 show this feature in action.

---

* Hint: do not actually move the location of the text objects, just swap their displayed text instead.

Step 20

5	1	2	3
9	10	6	
13	15	7	4
14	11	12	8

Step 27

9	5	1	2
13	10	6	3
14	15	7	4
	11	12	8

Fig. 6.5: Slide tile, continued

Step 60

9	2	10	6
14	15	13	1
5	12		8
11	3	4	7

Step 100

9	14	15	6
3	12	10	2
	13	7	8
5	11	4	1

Fig. 6.6: Slide tile, shuffled, now it is definitely a puzzle

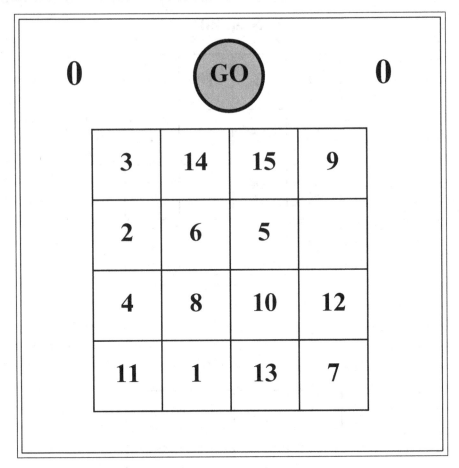

Fig. 6.7: Possible features, here a "go" button is used so that after a friend has shuffled the puzzle both a timer (left) and an update of total moves (right) can start

Lab615: Possible Features

Figure 6.7 shows one way a "game" feature could be implemented. We could also provide a shuffle button to make puzzles for us but be careful (!) to only use random legal moves; half of all states that result from generic shuffling are not reachable by sliding tiles (you would need to pop out one of the tiles, which is cheating).

If the tiles display words instead of numbers then be careful (!) again because repeated letters may not have interchangeable positions, and keeping track of which is which would be a real challenge (for the user). Figure 6.8 suggests a similar idea only using an image that was first broken into pieces with PIL. Also, we might keep track of the moves made and print them to a file so we can replay the game later.

Time 0   **Step 0**

Time 60   **Step 79**

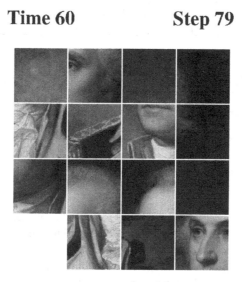

Fig. 6.8: Possible features, shuffle the broken-up pieces of an image using PIL (Image of George Washington courtesy of the U.S. Army, photo credit U.S. Army Military History Institute)

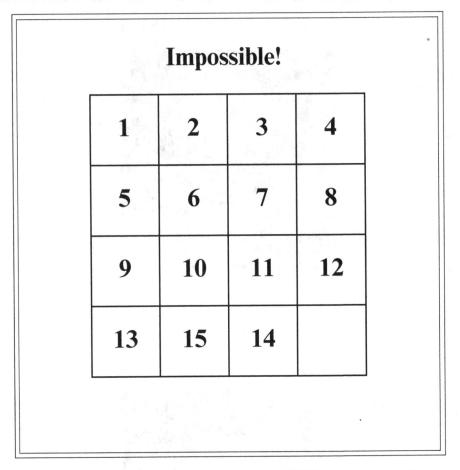

Impossible!

1	2	3	4
5	6	7	8
9	10	11	12
13	15	14	

Fig. 6.9: Impossible to solve, note that the 14 and 15 have been swapped

Million Dollar Prize

Two tiles are neighbors if the sum of the absolute value of their row difference and the absolute value of their column difference is equal to one.

Likewise, two *states* are neighbors if a single move transitions the 4×4 grid of tiles from one state to the other. While there are only $O(n^2)$ tiles in a grid there are an astronomical $O((n^2)!/2)$ states. For a 5×5 puzzles that translates to $O(10^{24})$. Computer search for any sequence of moves to solve a puzzle is thus very difficult but (!) a related problem is so important that it now has a very, *very* large prize:

http://www.claymath.org/millennium-problems/
p-vs-np-problem

The puzzle in Fig. 6.9 offered a similar prize in the 1800s, and sales were brisk!

6.2 Anagram Scramble

All results in this section reflect the use of the word list: `lab621.txt`

Lab621: Word in Word

Desired output is shown in Code Listing 6.2 where we identify four-letter words found in the middle of six-letter words. Code Listing 6.3 shows two options for storing the four-letter words, assuming they are pre-screened out of the word list.

When the user types a six-letter word we must check if the middle four characters also form a word. We might use the `in` operator to do this but with a list that will require a loop. (Even if we do not see the loop it still happens.) On the other hand, checking `in` with a hashtable does not use a loop because the hash function maps directly to the key in question. Really this is a *hash set* since only the keys matter.

Code Listing 6.2: Sample output highlighting embedded words

```
Six-letter word:   aching
aCHINg

Six-letter word:   coarse
cOARSe
Six-letter word:   modest
mODESt

Six-letter word:   sacred
sACREd

Six-letter word:   street
sTREEt
```

Code Listing 6.3: A loop to pre-screen the original word list

```
#
list4=[]
hash4={}
#
for word in wordlist:
    if len(word)==4:
    #
        list4.append(word)  # flat list
        hash4[word]=None    # hash set
    #
#
```

Lab622: Handshake Problem, Two Groups

We now find all pairs of four- and six-letter words where the middle of the longer word is the same as the shorter word. Partial output is shown in Code Listing 6.4. Our word list contains $O(5000)$ six-letter words and $O(1800)$ four-letter words.

Imagine that every six-letter word "shakes hands" with every four-letter word. This would total $O(5000 \times 1800) = O(9,000,000)$ handshakes. But of all those millions there are only $O(500)$ hits where we actually find one word inside another, less than a 0.01 % hit rate. This is what happens to our code if we store the four-letter words in a list because the in operator must check all of those words in a loop.

In the hashtable case the six-letter words do not shake hands with everyone but instead attempt to shake hands directly with a single four-letter word. This means there are now only $O(5000)$ handshakes and our hit rate goes up to 10 %, not bad!

Code Listing 6.5 shows the six-letter words shaking hands.

Code Listing 6.4: Partial output of all word-in-word matches

```
dROWSy
dWELLs
eLAPSe
eNAMEl
eQUIPs
eQUITy
eVENTs
fABLEd
fABLEs
fAKINg
fEASTs
fEVERs
fEWESt
fLAKEd
```

Code Listing 6.5: How many times do six-letter words shake hands?

```
#
for word in list6:
    #
    middle = ...
    #
    if middle in ...
        #
        print list6[0] + middle.upper() + list6[5]
        #
    #
#
```

Lab623: Anagrams

Example anagrams are shown in Code Listing 6.6, four-letter words only.

Code Listing 6.7 shows one way to directly check if two words are anagrams. One word is converted into a list of characters and then we loop over the characters in the other word. If at any point we find a character that does not match then we immediately return failure. When characters do match we must remove them from the character list otherwise we may fall into a common trap regarding duplicate letters: "rare" and "area" are not anagrams.

Only when all the letters have matched do we return success. Can you think of another way to find anagrams? Perhaps a more efficient way?

Code Listing 6.6: Sample output of four-letter anagrams

```
scar arcs

lamb balm

calm clam

team mate

slow owls

part trap

save vase
```

Code Listing 6.7: A direct check to see if two words are anagrams

```
#
def anagrams(word1,word2):
    #
    chlist=list(word1)
    #
    for ch in word2:
        #
        if ch not in chlist:
            return False
        else:
            chlist.remove(ch)
        #
    #
    return True
#
```

Lab624: Handshake Problem, One Group

We now find all pairs of four-letter words that are anagrams. Coincidentally, there are $O(500)$ such pairs. Algorithm 6.2.1 shows how to pair together all possible combinations of any two four-letter words. Note that the inner-loop does not reset to zero each time because the handshakes are always initiated by the word with the lower index in the word list, to avoid duplicate pairings.

Code Listings 6.8 and 6.9 suggest two indirect ways to check for anagrams. Namely, if two words are anagrams then they will have the same letter frequency tables and the same sorted letter strings. You can either import `lowercase` from the `string` module or just make a variable:

$$lowercase='abcdefghijklmnopqrstuvwxyz'$$

Algorithm 6.2.1 All-pairs handshaking within a single group

```
1: while j = 0, 1, 2, ... do
2:    while k = j + 1, j + 2, ... do
3:       if anagrams then
4:          print pair
5:       end if
6:    end while
7: end while
```

Code Listing 6.8: Calculating a letter frequency table for a word

```
def freqtable(word):
    #
    retval=[]
    for ch in lowercase:
        retval.append( word.count(ch) )
    return retval
#
```

Code Listing 6.9: Calculating a sorted letter string for a word

```
def sortedstring(word):
    #
    retval=''
    for ch in lowercase:
        for ltr in word:
            if ch==ltr:
                retval+=ch
    return retval
#
```

Lab625: Anagram Sets

Code Listing 6.10 shows a dramatic increase in algorithm efficiency. Rather than generating all possible pairs and checking each pair for anagrams, the code shown uses a word's sorted letter string as the key in a hashtable where the value is a list of all words who share that key. But those lists are precisely the anagram sets!

Compare this to what we previously saw in Lab412 and Lab413.

Only a single loop over the words is required but the code for building a sorted letter string could still be improved. That function loops over 26 letters in the alphabet and then 4 letters in a word, a total of $O(100)$ operations. Surely we can sort four letters with fewer than 100 operations. Even a bubble sort would work!

Code Listing 6.11 shows partial output of the sets found where the hash key was taken initially from the middle letters of a six-letter word, whether or not they formed a word themselves. This is meant to be suggestive of any number of common games that involve unscrambling jumbled words.

Of course in the general case we are not limited to the middle set or to only four letters. However, if our goal is to find all words that can be formed using *any* subset of letters then we must also be prepared to generate those subsets... recursion!

Code Listing 6.10: Hashing sets of anagrams into a common bin

```
#
htable={}
#
for word in list4:
    #
    key=sortedstring(word)
    if key not in htable:
        htable[key]=[]
    htable[key].append(word)
#
```

Code Listing 6.11: Partial output of anagram sets

```
beasts:   east eats sate seat teas
betide:   diet edit tide tied
demand:   amen mane mean name
devils:   evil live veil vile
gamete:   mate meat meta tame team
lapels:   leap pale peal plea
onsets:   nest nets sent tens
pseudo:   deus dues sued used
upsets:   pest pets sept step
```

Table 6.1: Example word ladders, letter substitution only

radius	spider	crafty
radios	slider	crafts
ratios	slicer	grafts
ration	slices	grants
nation	slicks	grands
notion	clicks	brands
motion	clucks	braids
		brains
		trains
		traits
		tracts
		traces
		braces
		braves
		braver
		beaver
		beater
		better
		batter
		fatter
		falter
		salter
		salver
		salves
		solves
		wolves

Word Ladder Puzzles

A word ladder is a type of puzzle where a starting and an ending word are specified and to solve the puzzle you must provide a list of intermediate words such that from one word to the next only the following changes may occur:

- Insert a letter.
- Delete a letter.
- Substitute a letter.
- Substitute the entire word for an anagram.

Table 6.1 shows puzzles where only the "substitute a letter" change is allowed but even here we may quickly face an exceedingly large search space once again.

Fig. 6.10: Final version, a beanbag cannon popping bubbles

6.3 Collision Detection

Jugglers often use beanbags in their performances because they are easy to handle and also safe if there should be any kind of accident.

Likewise, in Fig. 6.10 we show the final version of a game in which we launch beanbags to pop bubbles as they drift upward. We will build this game step-by-step and include the following features:

- Aiming the beanbag cannon by using the arrow keys to rotate left or right.
- Launch a beanbag by hitting spacebar. The beanbag moves linearly offscreen.
- Launch multiple beanbags in rapid succession but with a limited total number.
- Randomized bubbles that move up linearly but drift back-and-forth sideways.
- Detection of collisions between beanbags and bubbles... so the bubbles pop!

Safety First

Do not attempt to play this game in real life without permission and supervision.

Code Listing 6.12: Shell for part of a program to control a beanbag cannon

```
#
def leftarrow(evnt):
  global theta
  #
  theta += ...
  if theta > ... # stay within range
    theta = ...
  #
  ...
#
...
root.bind('<Left>' ,leftarrow)
root.bind('<Right>',rightarrow)
```

Lab631: Ready, Aim, Beanbag!

Code Listing 6.12 and Figs. 6.11–6.12 use arrow keys to aim a beanbag cannon.

Fig. 6.11: Aim beanbag cannon, do not allow θ to get too close to the horizontal

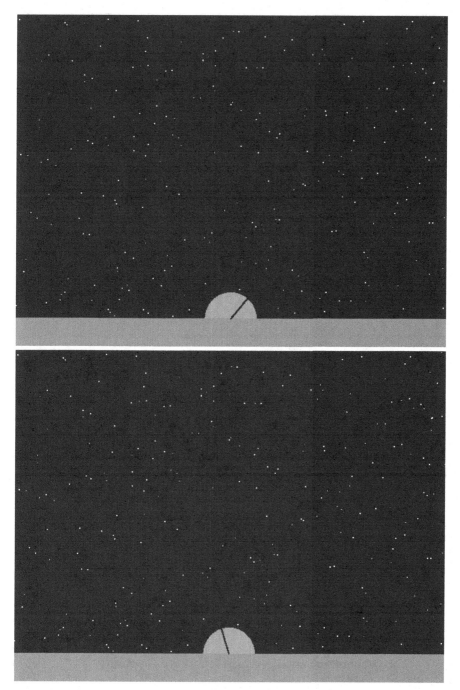

Fig. 6.12: Cannon moving. *Top*: First 45° right. *Bottom*: Then 15° over to the left

Fig. 6.13: Launch beanbag, a single flying object is created by pressing spacebar

Lab632: Launch Beanbag

Figure 6.13 and Code Listing 6.13 launch a single beanbag. If the object exists we do not launch another one. Code Listing 6.14 is the animation loop; our beanbag moves linearly and once offscreen we clear the Tk oval and reset obj=None. Access the class in Code Listing 6.15 using: from beanbag import Beanbag

Code Listing 6.13: Press the spacebar to launch a beanbag from the cannon

```
obj=None
#
def space(evt):
    global obj
    #
    if obj==None:
        xc,yc,xpos,ypos=cnvs.coords(cannon_aim)
        ...
        obj=Beanbag(xpos,ypos, ... , ... ,cnvs)
    #
#
```

Code Listing 6.14: Our beanbag object moves linearly across the screen

```
def tick():
    global obj
    #
    if obj!=None:
        if obj.offscreen():
            obj.delete_me()
            obj=None
        else:
            obj.move_me()
    #
    cnvs.after(1,tick)
#
```

Code Listing 6.15: Shell for the Beanbag class, filename: beanbag.py

```
class Beanbag:
    #
    def __init__(self,x,y,vx,vy,cnvs):
        #
        ...
        #
        self.r    = 5
        self.w    = int(cnvs.cget('width'))
        self.h    = int(cnvs.cget('height'))
        #
        self.tkid = cnvs.create_oval( ... )
        #
    #
    def offscreen(self):
        #
        ...
        #
    #
    def delete_me(self):
        #
        self.cnvs.delete(self.tkid)
        #
    #
    def move_me(self):
        #
        ...
        #
    #
#
```

Code Listing 6.16: A program both defining and using a Turtle class

```
#
from math import cos,sin,pi
#
class Turtle:
    #
    def __init__(self,x,y,h):
        #
        # instance variables
        #
        self.x = x
        self.y = y
        self.h = h
        #
    #
    def move(self,r):
        #
        oldx,oldy=self.x,self.y
        #
        self.x +=  r*cos(self.h*pi/180.0)
        self.y += -r*sin(self.h*pi/180.0)
        #
        drawline(oldx,oldy,self.x,self.y)
    #
    ...
    #
#
####################
#
# main program
#
smidge=Turtle(0,0,90)
smidge.move(100)
#
```

Scope

Code Listing 6.16 shows a class definition for Turtle, from Chap. 2, where instance data such as self.x are directly accessible by functions of the class (note the first argument of move is named self), thus the global command is unnecessary.

Local variables such as oldx occupy memory that is allocated for their use only during execution of the function. Once the function has ended then, as we have seen, that portion of the system call stack may be re-allocated for other data.

Fig. 6.14: List of beanbags, note how each trajectory is independent once launched

Lab633: List of Beanbags

First, the Beanbag class code does not change at all here. What has to change in the program to make multiple beanbags? Figure 6.14 and Code Listing 6.17 show how each beanbag knows its own position and velocity independently of the others.

Code Listing 6.17: Loop backward to avoid skipping over any beanbags

```
def tick():
    #
    j=len(objlist)-1
    while j>=0:
        #
        if objlist[j].offscreen():
            objlist[j].delete_me()
            objlist.pop(j)
        else:
            objlist[j].move_me()
        j-=1
    ...
```

Code Listing 6.18: Bubbles move up linearly but drift back-and-forth sideways

```
class Bubble:
    ...
    #
    def move_me(self):
        #
        if random()<0.5:
            self.x += self.vx*dt
        else:
            self.x -= self.vx*dt
        #
        self.y -= self.vy*dt
        ...
#
```

Lab634: Bubbles

Code Listing 6.18 and Figs. 6.15–6.16 show one bubble's movement, then many.

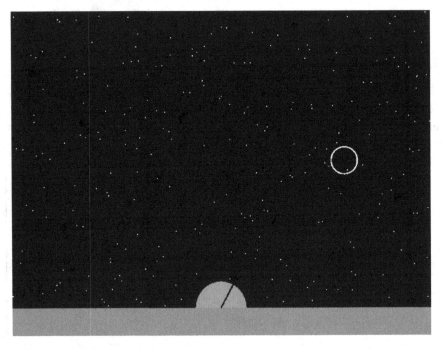

Fig. 6.15: Bubble drifts upward, where obviously we would prefer a list of them

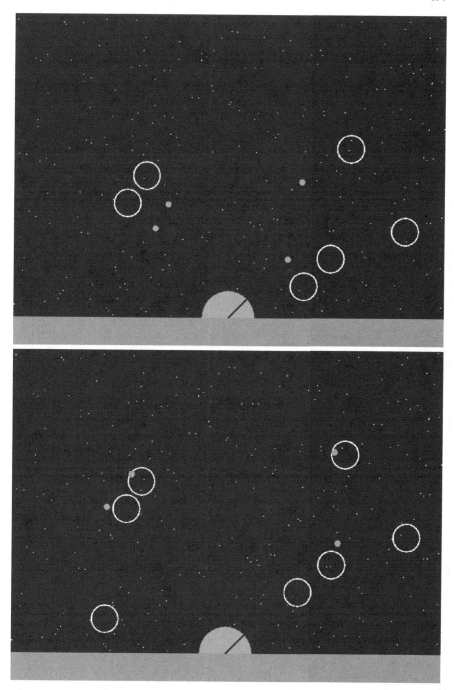

Fig. 6.16: List of bubbles, no collisions yet so the beanbags just fly right on by

Lab635: Collisions

We use circles because they are the easiest shape to code.

In this case we know the two positions (x_1, y_1) and (x_2, y_2) so by finding the distance between these points we can determine whether or not there is a collision. There will be a collision if that distance is less than the sum of the radius of the beanbag and the radius of the bubble.

Code Listing 6.19 shows the program's animation loop and Fig. 6.17 confirms our collision detection is working. For now Code Listing 6.20 shows the beanbag detecting a collision and, thus, accessing the bubble object's own position data.

Code Listing 6.19: Handshake problem, two groups: beanbags and bubbles

```
def tick():
    #
    ...
    #
    for obj in objlist: # beanbags do not pop
        #
        j=len(bubbles)-1
        while j>=0:
            #
            if obj.collide(bubbles[j]):
                #
                ...
                #
            j-=1
    ...
```

Code Listing 6.20: Beanbags are the ones detecting collisions, for now

```
class Beanbag:
    ...
    #
    def collide(self,the_bubble):
        #
        x1=self.x
        y1=self.y
        #
        x2=the_bubble.x
        y2=the_bubble.y
        #
        ...
#
```

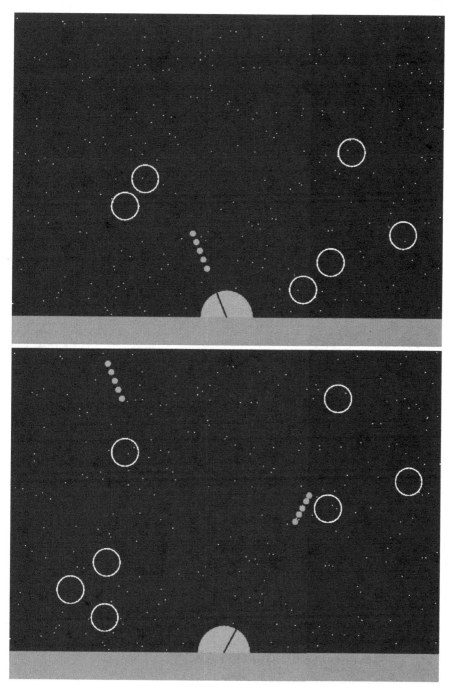

Fig. 6.17: Collisions, where clearly the bubbles hit by a beanbag now pop

Inheritance → Class Hierarchy

We might "re-factor" the common features of Beanbag and Bubble into a more generic type as Code Listing 6.21 shows, where collide is now defined in the new class FlyingObject instead of in Beanbag.

Code Listing 6.22 and Code Listing 6.23 show how to inherit these features in our existing classes, as well as how to specify those distinctions that still remain between the sub-classes. Note how the super-class constructor is explicitly called.

Code Listing 6.21: Shell for super-class FlyingObject

```
class FlyingObject:
    #
    def __init__(self, ...radius,fill,outline,width):
        #
        # instance variables
        #
        ...
        #
        self.tkid = cnvs.create_oval( ... )
        #
    def offscreen(self):
        #
        ...
        #
    def delete_me(self):
        #
        self.cnvs.delete(self.tkid)
        #
    def collide(self,the_other_flying_object):
        #
        x1=self.x
        y1=self.y
        #
        x2=the_other_flying_object.x
        y2=the_other_flying_object.y
        #
        ...
        #
    def update(self):
        #
        self.cnvs.coords(self.tkid, ... )
        #
#
```

Code Listing 6.22: Shell for sub-class Beanbag "isa" FlyingObject

```
#
from flyingObject import FlyingObject
#
class Beanbag(FlyingObject):
    #
    def __init__(self,x,y,vx,vy,cnvs):
        #
        FlyingObject.__init__(self, ...5,'gray','gray',1)
        #
    def move_me(self):
        #
        ...
        #
        self.update()
        #
#
```

Code Listing 6.23: Shell for sub-class Bubble "isa" FlyingObject

```
#
from flyingObject import FlyingObject
#
from random import random
#
class Bubble(FlyingObject):
    #
    def __init__(self,x,y,cnvs):
        #
        FlyingObject.__init__(self, ...25,None,'white',2)
        #
    def move_me(self):
        #
        if random()<0.5:
            self.x += self.vx*dt
        else:
            self.x -= self.vx*dt
        #
        self.y -= self.vy*dt
        #
        self.update()
        #
#
```

Fig. 6.18: Keeping score. The giant seven is the number of bubbles popped so far

Keeping Score

Figure 6.18 and Code Listing 6.24 show one way to keep score. Alternatively, since the beanbags themselves do not pop, we might add a bonus every time a beanbag pops more than one bubble: two points for the second bubble, four points for the third, then eight, sixteen, and so on. We can count misses, too, but a beanbag missing all the bubbles is not the same as a bubble having been missed by all the beanbags.

Statistics could also include the ratio of hits to beanbags launched, and the percentage of bubbles popped. We might "turn on" gravity and air resistance, and wind, then offer higher point values for popping bubbles in more challenging conditions.

Code Listing 6.24: Keeping score by counting the number of bubbles popped

```
#
if obj.collide(bubbles[j]):
    #
    ...
    #
    myScore += 1
    cnvs.itemconfigure(txt,text='%d'%myScore)
```

Chapter 7
Modeling, Part I

Figure 7.1 shows an event in which our sun ejects hundreds of billions of pounds of material at temperatures as high as tens of millions of degrees and moving at speeds as fast as a couple million miles per hour, toward us.

http://helios.gsfc.nasa.gov/cme.html

After a few days the material arrives at Earth where it can cause all kinds of problems to our technological infrastructure, particularly those systems we have in orbit. Dr. Eric R. Christian, from NASA, described it as being like a "billion hydrogen bombs" exploding. And this from the body upon which all our life depends!

Figure 7.2 on the next page shows how we have always responded to living in such a dangerous universe. We press on. We work to understand and to overcome, and a *computational model* is one way we study interactions with the physical world.

Fig. 7.1: A coronal mass ejection on 20 June 2013 (Image courtesy of NASA)

© Springer International Publishing 2016
S. Torbert, *Applied Computer Science*, DOI 10.1007/978-3-319-30866-1_7

Fig. 7.2: Engineering systems. From *top left*: power lines, pipeline, dam, bridge, quarry, shipping port, canal, submarine. We choose to take the world not simply as it is but as we might make it to be. We do this with great risk and also patience. Models provide information, and information accelerates the discovery of improved solutions. Over time computational models have supplanted other forms of testing, not as the final word but as a guide in its direction (Images courtesy of Pixabay)

7.1 Laws of Motion

We use Newton's second law of motion in the context of springs.

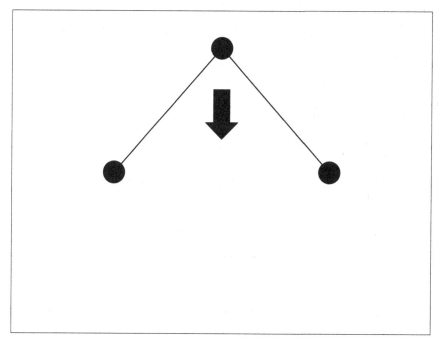

Fig. 7.3: Knobs attached to "springs" but only the middle knob moves, for now

Code Listing 7.1: Acceleration is based on vertical position (displacement) only

```
class Knob:
    def __init__(self,x,y,cnvs):
        ...
        self.vy=0
    #
    def move_me(self,knobLeft,knobRight):
        #
        yT = 0.5*(knobLeft.y+knobRight.y)
        #
        ay = 0.1*(yT-self.y)  # ad hoc "spring" constant
        #
        self.vy +=      ay*dt # timestep
        self.y  += self.vy*dt
        ...
```

Lab711: Hooke's Law

Code Listings 7.1 and 7.2 show a generic "knob" and Figs. 7.3, 7.4, and 7.5 show its motion over time. We calculate acceleration (Hooke and Newton) based on vertical displacement from a desired position halfway between the two neighbors.

Code Listing 7.2: Shell of a program that uses three knob objects

```
def tick():
    #
    knob2.move_me(knob1,knob3) # only knob2 moves
    #
    cnvs.coords(tkid1, ... ,knob1.y, ... ,knob2.y)
    ...
#
knob1=Knob( ... , ... ,cnvs)
knob2=Knob( ... , ... ,cnvs) # vertical displacement
knob3=Knob( ... , ... ,cnvs)
#
tkid1=cnvs.create_line( ... ,fill='black',width=2)
tkid2=cnvs.create_line( ... ,fill='black',width=2)
```

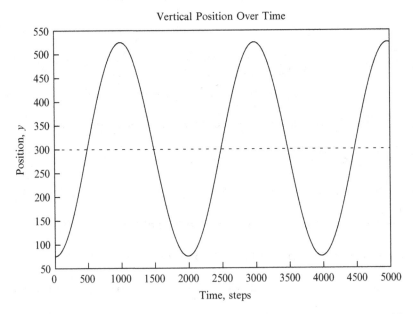

Fig. 7.4: Vertical position of the middle knob as it oscillates between its neighbors

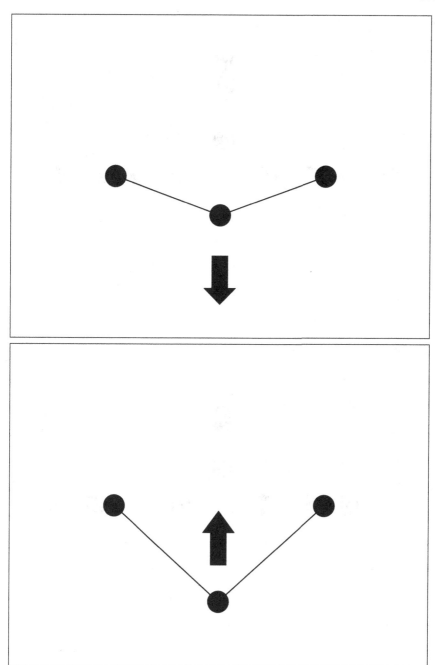

Fig. 7.5: Hooke's Law, motion governed by displacement and a spring constant

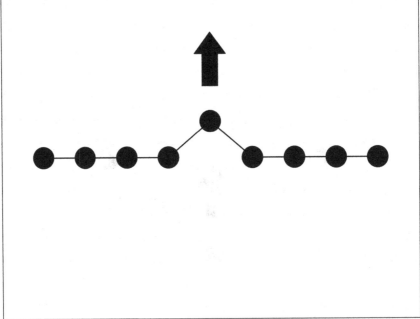

Fig. 7.6: Hooke's Law, without the *arrow* we could not determine which direction
the knob is moving. *Top*: shortly after the start. *Bottom*: later at the same *y* position

Lab712: Chain of Knobs

Figures 7.6 and 7.7 again show a single knob moving but now we have an entire list of objects, as shown in Code Listing 7.3, and next almost all of them will move too.

Code Listing 7.3: A list of knobs but still only the middle knob is moving

```
def tick():
    #
    knobs[4].move_me(knobs[3],knobs[5]) # middle knob
    #
    # also re-draw the springs connected to this knob
    #
#
j=0
while j<9:
    #
    # j==4 ... vertical displacement
    #
    knobs.append( Knob( ... , ... ,cnvs) )
    j+=1
```

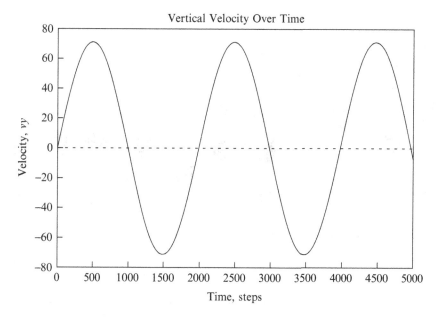

Fig. 7.7: Vertical velocity of the middle knob as it oscillates between its neighbors

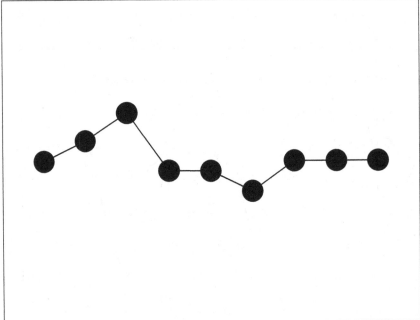

Fig. 7.8: Hooke's Law, depending on which knobs are fixed in place an asymmetry can be established. *Top*: shortly after the start. *Bottom*: later we see a new pattern

Lab713: Asymmetry

Figures 7.8 and 7.9, and Code Listing 7.4, show multiple knobs moving. Since the fixed knobs and the initialization are asymmetric an "interesting" sequence unfolds.

We might also connect four nearest neighbors in 2-D (or six in 3-D) to model a cloth mesh or even solid objects. This suggests the possibility of using computer modeling in the real-time development of industrial products where, for instance, simulation could limit the amount of time wasted re-shipping prototypes.

Code Listing 7.4: Two endpoints are fixed, plus the next two knobs on the right

```
def tick():
    #
    j=1
    while j<6:
        #
        knobs[j].move_me(knobs[j-1],knobs[j+1])
        j+=1
    ...
```

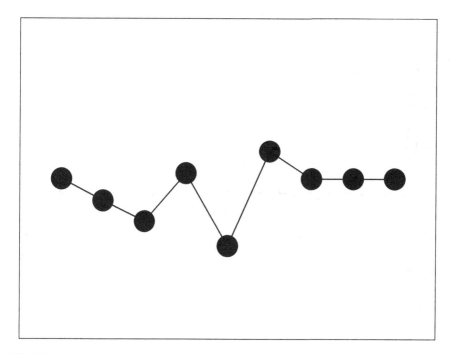

Fig. 7.9: Hooke's Law, continued, even later. Each knob has the same desire to move between its two nearest neighbors except, now, they are also moving themselves

Lab714: Damping

Figures 7.10 and 7.11 show many more knobs and an extreme initial displacement. The result is a wave that propagates first to the right and then back left. It would continue reflecting back-and-forth forever except that Code Listing 7.5 adds a damping term to a_y so that the "chain" will eventually settle down.

Code Listing 7.5: A damping term added to each knob's acceleration calculation

```
class Knob:
    ...
    def move_me(self,knobLeft,knobRight):
        #
        yT = 0.5*(knobLeft.y+knobRight.y)
        #
        ay = 0.1*(yT-self.y)-0.5*self.vy # ad hoc damping
        #
        self.vy +=       ay*dt
        self.y  += self.vy*dt
        ...
```

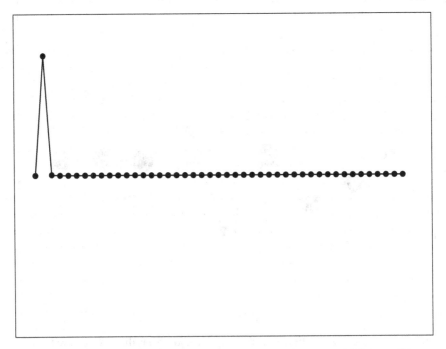

Fig. 7.10: Hooke's Law plus damping, fixed ends and extreme initial conditions

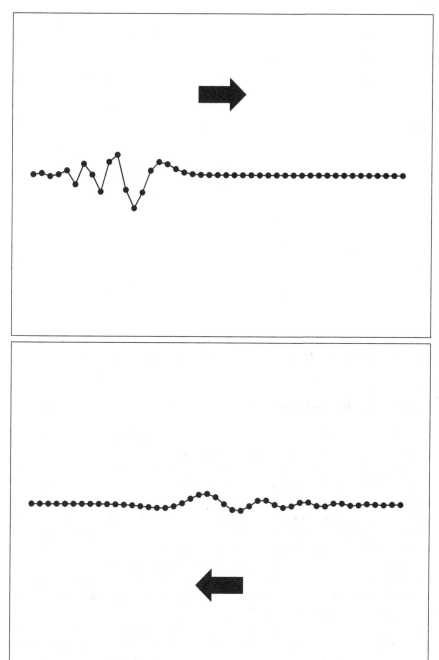

Fig. 7.11: Hooke's Law plus damping, continued, a wave pattern emerges and then propagates back-and-forth. *Top*: shortly after the start. *Bottom*: later, now returning

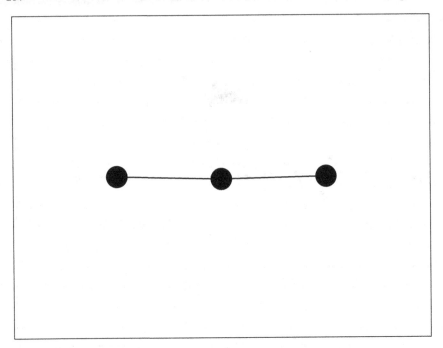

Fig. 7.12: Only the middle knob moves, again, but with damping. After 5000 steps

Original Case with Damping

To illustrate the effect of damping we return to the original example of three knobs attached to springs where only the middle knob moved.

In the first instance the middle knob would oscillate between its two neighbors indefinitely. The patterns shown over time for both the position and velocity of the moving knob were periodic.

In contrast, Fig. 7.12 shows that with damping "turned on" the middle knob will eventually come to rest with position equal to the desired target (the average position of its neighbors) and velocity equal to zero.

Likewise in Fig. 7.13 we see that both the position and velocity are no longer periodic but rather, instead, approach these final values. Had we waited more time in Lab724 then its wave pattern would have disappeared, too, like an ocean wave that disappears when it reaches the beach.

Also compare the additional damping term here with the air resistance term added to the projectile model in Lab123. The projectile was not connected to any other object by a spring but it was influenced by gravity, to be added again next.

Fig. 7.13: Vertical position and velocity of the middle knob as it oscillates between its neighbors. *Top*: Position, coming to rest at the average of the two neighbors. *Bottom*: Velocity, approaching zero as the knob "comes to rest"

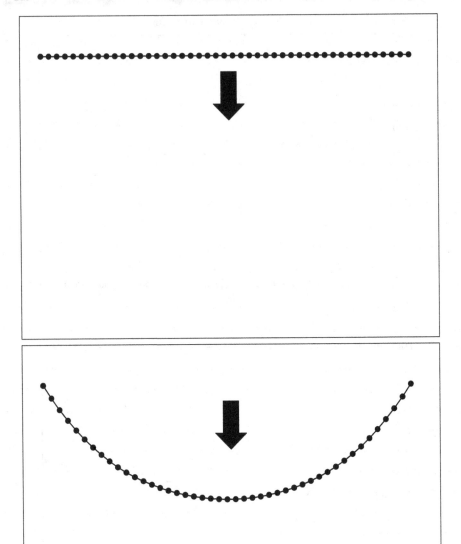

Fig. 7.14: Hooke's Law plus damping and gravity, fixed ends. *Top*: initial conditions. *Bottom*: after the start, gravity has caused the (symmetric) vertical displacements

Lab715: Gravity

Code Listing 7.6 now adds an ad hoc gravity term to our ad hoc spring plus ad hoc damping calculation. In this case, without gravity there would be no motion because the initial conditions do not include any displacement. The two end-knobs are still fixed in place and Figs. 7.14 and 7.15 show motion toward a steady state.

Code Listing 7.6: A gravity term added to each knob's acceleration calculation

```
class Knob:
    ...
    def move_me(self,knobLeft,knobRight):
        #
        yT = 0.5*(knobLeft.y+knobRight.y)
        #
        ay = 10.0*(yT-self.y)-0.5*self.vy+10.0 # ad hoc
        #
        self.vy +=        ay*dt
        self.y  += self.vy*dt
        ...
```

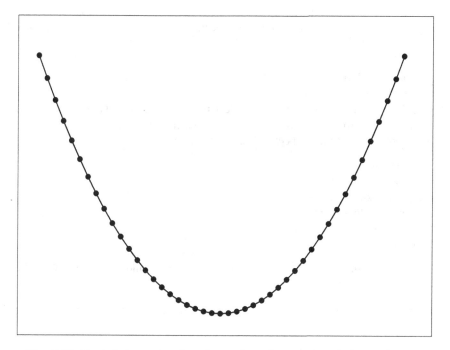

Fig. 7.15: Hooke's Law plus damping and gravity, continued. At steady state

Fig. 7.16: U.S. Navy carrier group in the Pacific Ocean (Image courtesy of the U.S. Navy, photo credit Mass Communication Specialist 2nd Class Walter M. Wayman)

A Technological World

Figure 7.16 shows one way nations project power around the world. It is not an insignificant task to develop, build, and maintain a carrier group.

Consider the following aspects of these operations...

- Hull design.
- Navigation and control.
- Weapon systems.
- On-board defensive measures.
- Communication.
- Communication security.

... and in each instance a computational model, of one kind or another, might be used to discover1 a more efficient, more reliable, more effective solution.

7.2 Collisions in 1-D

Consider an idealized physical system in which collisions between two objects, which we will call "blocks," are perfectly elastic. When blocks A and B collide then both their velocities change. If the mass of block A is m_A and its velocity is v_A, and similarly m_B and v_B for B, then...

$$v_a = v_A$$
$$v_b = v_B$$

$$v_A = \frac{v_a\,(m_A - m_B) + 2m_B v_b}{m_A + m_B}$$

$$v_B = \frac{v_b\,(m_B - m_A) + 2m_A v_a}{m_A + m_B}$$

... are the new velocities.

Temporary variables are used for the original velocities because in reality the physical changes happen simultaneously whereas the commands issued to a computer are sequential, and we do not want the new value of v_A to be used to calculate the new value of v_B. The old value of v_A, called v_a, should be used.

In one dimension the direction is only right or left, and so a positive velocity indicates a block moving right while a negative sign is for moving left.

A special case is the collision of two blocks with the same mass, $m_B = m_A$. Then, the formulas from above will reduce to a simple exchange, or swap.

$$v_A = v_b$$
$$v_B = v_a$$

Another special case is when one block is a "wall" with $v_B = 0$ and $m_B \gg m_A$.

$$v_A = -v_a$$
$$v_B = 0$$

We begin with a single block bouncing off a wall, then examine two blocks with the same mass colliding, followed by a smaller block bouncing off a larger block, and then a sequence of ever-larger blocks hitting into a smaller one.

Our results may be presented both as an animation of the motion of the blocks and as an analysis of their positions and velocities over time. Even though the animations are drawn in 2-D all of the interactions are modeled in only 1-D. The next problem will consider the truly two-dimensional case.

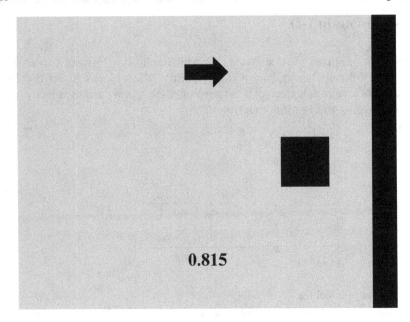

0.815

Fig. 7.17: Bounce block. Approaching the wall at time $t = 0.815$ seconds

Lab721: Bounce Block

Figure 7.17 shows a snapshot from the animation of a block moving to the right at time $t = 0.815$ seconds. The initial velocity of the block is 250 pixels per second and the initial position (of the center of the block) is 100 pixels measured from the left side of the screen.

The width of the wall on the right side of the screen is 25 pixels and the block is drawn as a square with side-length 50 pixels. Since the dimensions of the screen are 400×300 the block will hit the wall when $x = 350$ pixels. (The screen height does not influence the block at all because the problem is, in fact, one-dimensional.)

Figure 7.18 shows position and velocity as they change over time. The motion of the block is *linear* since there is no gravity, no wind, no air resistance, no spring, and no damping. The only change to v is when its direction turns from positive to negative, at the instant the block hits the wall. The plot of (t, v) shows this as a sudden "step" from 250 down to -250 pixels per second, when (t, x) is at its peak.

The point marked in each plot corresponds to the snapshot from the animation. Both before and after its collision with the wall the motion of the block is described by a linear change in x and a constant v. After $t = 2.5$ seconds have elapsed the block will completely disappear off the left side of the screen and never return.

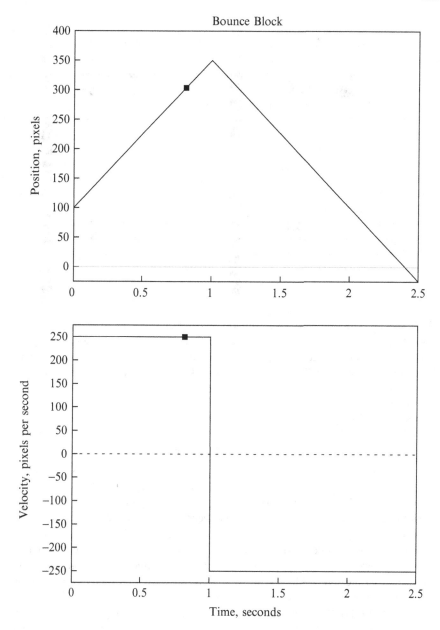

Fig. 7.18: Bounce block. *Top*: position *x*. *Bottom*: velocity *v*. At time $t = $ one second the block hits the wall and *v* instantaneously changes from 250 to -250 pixels per second. The point marked in both plots is $t = 0.815$ seconds, as shown previously

Fig. 7.19: Two blocks. Clockwise from top-left: block A moving right, post-collision block B moving right, B now moving left, post-collision again A now moving left and about to go off screen. Not counting the instance when block B hits the wall these are the only two collisions, and we can calculate the exact time of each

Lab722: Two Blocks

Figure 7.19 shows snapshots from the animation of two blocks A and B interacting. At time $t = 0.0$ seconds block B is not moving, so $v_B = 0$, and block A approaches B's position from the left (i.e., moving right). They have the same mass.

When block A collides with B it stops and $v_A = 0$, while block B then moves toward the wall at the same speed as A had been moving. Block B bounces off the wall in the manner seen previously and approaches A's position from the right.

When block B collides with A it stops and $v_B = 0$ again, while block A then moves away at its original speed but now in the other direction. After it disappears off the side of the screen block A never returns, so there are exactly two collisions between the blocks.

Figure 7.20 shows both positions and velocities as they change over time. In the plot showing (t,x), at the top, the 50 pixel gap between positions at $t = 1.0$ and $t = 3.0$ is due to a block's thickness and the fact that position is identified at the center of each square.

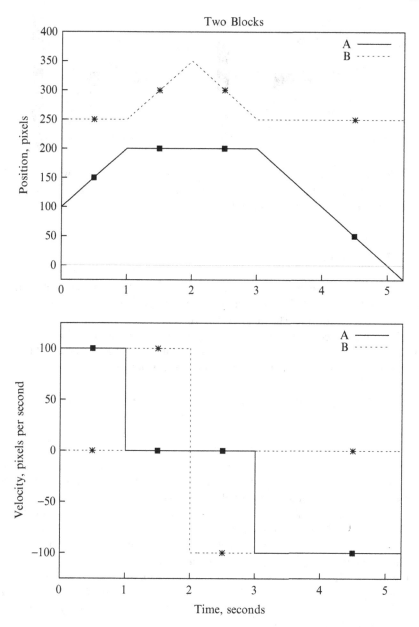

Fig. 7.20: Two blocks. *Top*: two positions x_A and x_B. *Bottom*: velocities v_A and v_B. Points marked in both plots correspond to the four snapshots shown previously

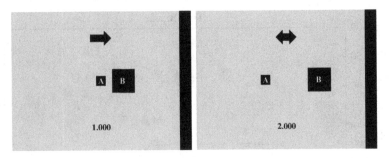

Fig. 7.21: Mass ratio. *Left*: block A moving right, about to collide with block B. *Right*: post-collision, block A moving left and block B moving right. B will not hit the wall before A goes off screen, and the two blocks will never collide again

Lab723: Mass Ratio

Figure 7.21 shows snapshots from the animation of two blocks A and B interacting. At time $t = 0.0$ seconds block B is not moving, so $v_B = 0$, and block A approaches B's position from the left. The mass of A is 16% the mass of B.

When block A collides with B it does not stop, as before, but instead bounces backward and moves left. Block B moves toward the wall at a slower speed than A had been moving and also at a slower speed than A is now moving.

$$v_A = \frac{v_a(m_A - m_B)}{m_A + m_B}$$

$$v_B = \frac{2m_A v_a}{m_A + m_B}$$

Block B will eventually bounce off the wall in the manner seen previously and then approach A's position from the right. However, block A will have already gone off screen by the time this happens and, more importantly, the speed of B will still be slower than the speed of A.

This means that block B will not catch up to block A and the two will never again collide. There is exactly one collision between the blocks.

Figure 7.22 shows both positions and velocities as they change over time. In the plot showing (t, x), at the top, block A is shown with a steeper slope than block B after they collide. Likewise, in the plot showing (t, v), at the bottom, the final speed of A is greater than the final speed of B.

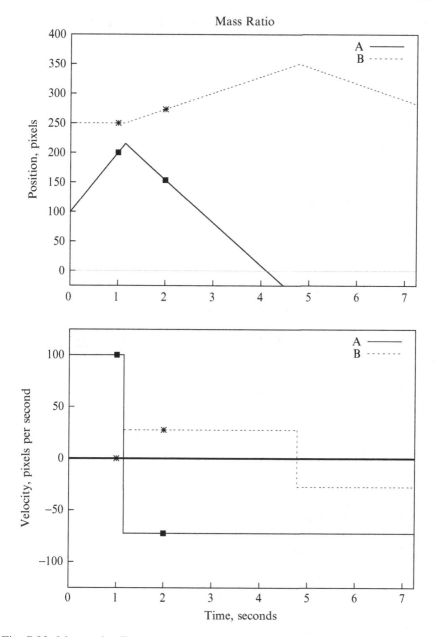

Fig. 7.22: Mass ratio. *Top*: two positions x_A and x_B. *Bottom*: velocities v_A and v_B. Points marked in both plots correspond to the two snapshots shown previously

Code Listing 7.7: Time step for a single block bouncing off a wall

```
#
def tick():
    global t,x,v
    #
    t +=    dt
    #
    x += v*dt
    #
    cnvs.coords(tkid, ... )
    #
    if ... and v>0:
        #
        v *= -1
        #
    #
    cnvs.after(1,tick)
#
```

Code Listing 7.8: Time step for two blocks A and B interacting

```
#
def tick():
    global t,xA,vA,xB,vB
    #
    t   +=    dt
    #
    xA += vA*dt
    xB += vB*dt
    #
    cnvs.coords(tkidA, ... )
    cnvs.coords(tkidB, ... )
    #
    if ... and vA>vB:
        #
        # collision between the blocks
        #
    #
    if ... and vB>0:
        #
        # block B bounces off the wall
        #
    #
    cnvs.after(1,tick)
#
```

Tick Function

Code Listing 7.7 shows one block bouncing off a wall and Code Listing 7.8 shows two blocks interacting. Each call to tick updates the position x based on the current velocity v and the incremental time step dt.

As an alternative, Code Listing 7.9 calculates when, in the future, the two blocks will collide and also when block B hits the wall. (This is possible because their motion is linear.) Whichever happens sooner is the ending time of our next interval.

Tick, then, does not use dt to update position. Instead we use the total elapsed time for the current interval and interpolate from starting position to ending position. When the interval ends we update position and, depending on which event occurred, change the velocities. Finally, we calculate the ending time for the next interval.

Code Listing 7.9: Interpolation for two blocks A and B interacting

```
#
def tick():
    global t,xA,vA,xB,vB
    #
    t   += dt
    #
    txA = xA + vA*(t-t0)  # interpolate
    txB = xB + vB*(t-t0)
    #
    # ...
    #
    if t>=t1:
        #
        xA += vA*(t1-t0)   # distance = rate * time
        xB += vB*(t1-t0)
        #
        # update velocities vA and/or vB
        #
        # ...
        #
        t0   = t1
        t1 += min( tBlocksHit , tBounceWall )
        #
    #
    cnvs.after(1,tick)
#
# ...
#
t0 = 0.0
t1 = min( tBlocksHit , tBounceWall )
#
```

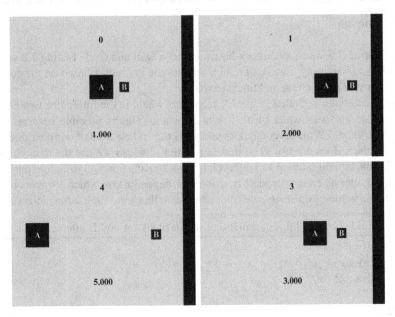

Fig. 7.23: Count collisions. Clockwise from top-left: block A moving right prior to the first collision, post-collision A is still moving right but slower than before and B is now moving left after having hit the wall, later both move left but B is faster, finally A is faster than B and so they never collide again. Four collisions in total

Lab724: Count Collisions

Figure 7.23 shows snapshots from the animation of two blocks A and B interacting. At time $t = 0.0$ seconds block B is not moving, so $v_B = 0$, and block A approaches B's position from the left. The mass of B is 16% the mass of A. The number at the top-middle of each snapshot counts the total collisions between the blocks.

When A collides with B it does not stop, as before, nor does it bounce backward. Instead block A continues moving right but at a slower speed, even as B moves right at a faster speed, appearing to "chase" it toward the wall.

Block B hits the wall and then approaches A's position from the right. When the blocks collide again A will slow down but still continue moving right. Block A will chase B toward the wall again and the two will eventually collide again.

Each time the blocks collide A will slow down. After the third collision A is moving left and after the fourth collision it is moving faster than B.

Figure 7.24 shows both positions and velocities as they change over time. In the plot showing (t, x), at the top, block A is shown with a steeper slope than block B after the fourth collision. Likewise, in the plot showing (t, v), at the bottom, the final speed of A is greater than the final speed of B.

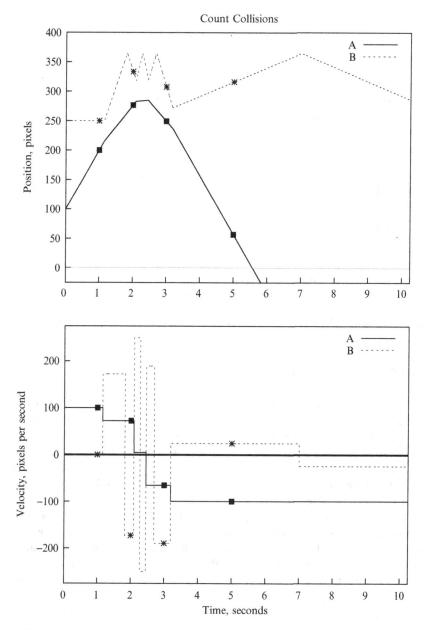

Fig. 7.24: Count collisions. *Top*: two positions x_A and x_B. *Bottom*: velocities v_A and v_B. Points marked in both plots correspond to the four snapshots shown previously. Block A slows down after each collision and only changes its direction one time. Block B changes direction every time it hits either block A or the wall

Plot Collision Count

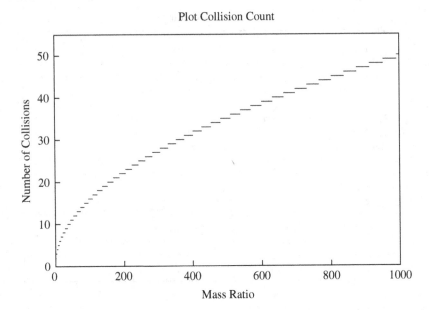

Fig. 7.25: Plot collision count. Observe that each count is necessarily an integer

Lab725: Plot Collision Count

Figure 7.25 shows the number of collisions between blocks A and B for various mass ratios. When the masses are the same the ratio is 1.0 and when the mass of A is smaller than the mass of B the ratio is less than 1.0. Almost all of the mass ratios shown are greater than 1.0 meaning the mass of A is greater than the mass of B.

Keep in mind that each collision count is an integer, and yet compare the shape of this plot with those shown previously in Lab322. Many thanks to Dr. John Dell for this fascinating observation.

Code Listing 7.10 shows the stopping criteria used for each different mass ratio. No time step or tick function is used. Instead, the intervals calculated previously for interpolation are used and "time" is advanced instantly to the end of each interval, since no animation is needed to calculate the count. Time intervals continue until the stopping criteria is satisfied, and the count increments whenever there is a collision.

Code Listing 7.10: Stopping criteria for the time loop used for each mass ratio

```
#
if  vA<0.0  and  vB>=0.0  and  -vA>vB:  break
if  vA<0.0  and  vB< 0.0  and   vA<vB:  break
#
```

7.3 Collisions in 2-D

Consider an idealized physical system in which collisions between two objects, which we will call "marbles," are perfectly elastic. When marbles collide then both their velocities change. Velocity v has two perpendicular components v_x and v_y.

If the masses are the same and their velocities *in the direction of the collision* are u_1 and u_2, then the effect of the collision is to exchange u_1 and u_2. (For different masses we would use the formula from the previous problem.) Likewise if a marble hits a wall, of any shape, then set $u_1 = -u_1$ in the direction of that collision.

Also, the marble's actual velocity v consists of a component w perpendicular to the axis of collision (i.e., perpendicular to u) and w does not change. So for each calculation our plan is to write v in terms of u and w, change u, and rebuild v.

Lab731: Bounce Marble

Figure 7.26 shows two photographs involving marbles, an ancient and a modern toy, used by humans everywhere for thousands of years.

Figure 7.27 on the following page shows a single marble's position and velocity as it bounces alone. The screen size is 400×300 and the marble begins at $(25, 275)$ with a velocity of $(100, -100)$ measured in pixels per second. Its radius is 25 pixels.

The times when the marble first bounces off the top wall and also when it first bounces off the side are marked in both the velocity plot and the position plot. Arrows indicate the direction of motion in the position plot and correspond to the velocity of the marble at that same time.

Code Listing 7.11 shows the shell of a program to move a single marble, using a class Marble to represent the object's position and velocity. A function call updates the marble over an incremental time step and changes its velocity whenever a collision occurs. Figure 7.28 shows the beginning of the actual animation where the pattern of motion repeats itself due to the simplicity of the circumstances.

Fig. 7.26: Marble toys. *Left*: A jar of marbles. *Right*: The ruins of Mohenjo-daro, where ancient marbles some 4000 years old have been found, in the Indus Valley (Images courtesy of Pixabay and Maqbool Ghanghro)

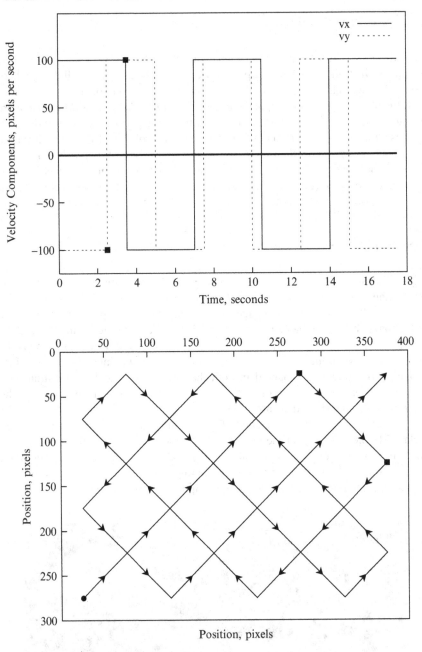

Fig. 7.27: Bounce marble. *Top*: velocity components. *Bottom*: position

Code Listing 7.11: Shell of a program to move a marble, using a class Marble

```
#
from Tkinter import Tk,Canvas
#
def tick():
    #
    marble.move_me(dt)
    #
    cnvs.after(1,tick)
#
root=Tk()
cnvs=Canvas(root,width=w,height=h)
cnvs.pack()
#
marble=Marble(cnvs)
#
cnvs.after(1,tick)
root.mainloop()
#
```

Fig. 7.28: A single marble where the pattern of motion will repeat itself

Code Listing 7.12: The definition of a Marble class to represent a marble

```
#
class Marble:
    #
    def __init__(self,cnvs):
        #
        self.cnvs = cnvs
        #
        self.w      = int(self.cnvs.cget('width'))
        self.h      = int(self.cnvs.cget('height'))
        #
        self.r    =   25.0 # pixels
        #
        self.x    =   25.0 # pixels
        self.y    =  275.0
        #
        self.vx   =  100.0 # pixels per second
        self.vy   = -100.0
        #
        self.tkid = self.cnvs.create_oval(\
                            self.x-self.r,\
                            self.y-self.r,\
                            self.x+self.r,\
                            self.y+self.r,\
                            fill=None,\
                            outline='black',width=3)
    #
    def move_me(self,dt):
        #
        self.x += (self.vx*dt)
        self.y += (self.vy*dt)
        #
        self.cnvs.coords(self.tkid,\
                        self.x-self.r,self.y-self.r,\
                        self.x+self.r,self.y+self.r)
        #
        if self.x+self.r>=self.w:
            #
            self.vx *= -1.0                 # u=vx and w=vy
            self.x    = self.w-self.r
            #
        #
        ...
    #
```

Lab732: List of Marbles

Code Listing 7.12 shows the special case where walls are only vertical, so $u = v_x$ and $w = v_y$. There is no need then to rewrite v or, after the bounce, to rebuild v anew. The same is true for horizontal walls where $u = v_y$ and $w = v_x$.

Code Listing 7.13 shows the random initialization of a marble object's velocity components. Rather than create a single Marble instance in our main program we will instead create a list and fill it with some number of Marble objects. If each such object had set the same velocity then they would all move on top of one another, visually indistinguishable.

Figure 7.29 shows eight marbles starting to move, spreading out, and separating. These marbles are only colliding with the walls and not with each other, for now.

Code Listing 7.13: Random initialization of a marble object's velocity components

```
#
from random import random
#
self.vx = 50.0 * random() + 50.0 # pixels per second
self.vy = 50.0 * random() + 50.0
#
```

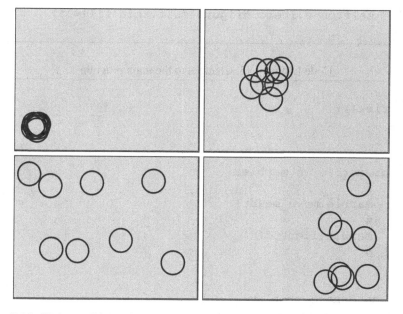

Fig. 7.29: Eight marbles. Clockwise from top-left: starting positions are the same but velocities are different, spreading out, after bouncing off the walls, separation

Code Listing 7.14: Additions to the Marble class

```
#
class Marble:
    #
    ...
    #
    def collide(self,the_other_marble):
        #
        dx = self.x - the_other_marble.x
        dy = self.y - the_other_marble.y
        #
        # find the distance between marbles
        #
        # check it using radius... return True or False
        #
    #
    def lightOn(self):
        #
        self.cnvs.itemconfigure(self.tkid,fill='black')
    #
    def lightOff(self):
        #
        self.cnvs.itemconfigure(self.tkid,fill='')
    #
```

Code Listing 7.15: Changes to the main program

```
#
def tick():
    #
    ...
    #
    for marble in marbles:
        #
        marble.move_me(dt)
        #
        marble.lightOff()
        #
    #
    #
    # handshake problem
    #
    # if collision then turn light on
    #
```

Lab733: Light On Light Off

Code Listing 7.14 shows three new functions in the Marble class.

Similar to cases in previously seen classes, we need to determine if two marbles have collided. Since the objects have been represented as circles this is a straightforward calculation: find the distance between marbles and check it using the radius. If the distance d is smaller than the sum $(r_1 + r_2)$ then the marbles are colliding and our function should return True. Otherwise return False.

The other two new functions control the display of a marble on the screen, either filled-in if the light is on or outline-only if the light is off.

Code Listing 7.15 shows changes to the main program that use these functions. First, at the beginning of each time step we turn all the lights off. Then, check for a collision between any possible pair and whenever we find two marbles have collided turn both of their lights on.

In this way our collision detection is visually confirmed. While the animation is running, any time two marbles happen to collide their change in appearance will indicate that our code is "aware" of what has happened. Likewise, when they separate again we will see that, too. Figure 7.30 shows four snapshots from the animation.

At this point the marble objects need just one step more in order to react fully to a collision: we now know the collision has happened and between which two marbles, all we need to do is change their velocities as a result.

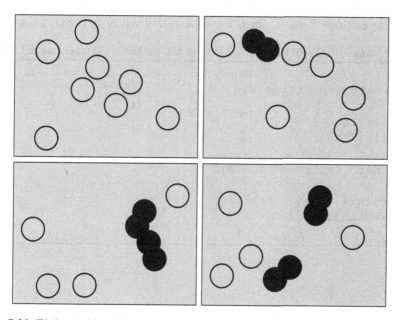

Fig. 7.30: Eight marbles. Clockwise from top-left: no collisions, a single pair of colliding marbles, two different collision pairs, and four marbles colliding all together

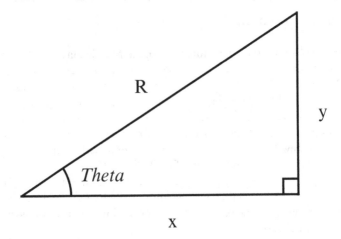

Fig. 7.31: Right triangle. When we know *x* and *y* then we can calculate *R* and θ

Right Triangle

Figure 7.31 and Code Listing 7.16 show four relationships we will find in *any* right triangle. That means if one of the three angles in the triangle measures 90°, or $\pi/2$ radians, then these four formulas will work. We can either calculate *x* and *y* or we can calculate *R* and θ, depending on the pair of values we already know.

Code Listing 7.16: Right triangle. Whichever two we know, the others we calculate

```
#
from math import cos,sin
#
x=R*cos(Theta)
y=R*sin(Theta)
#
from math import sqrt,atan2
#
R=sqrt(x*x + y*y)
Theta=atan2(y, x)
#
```

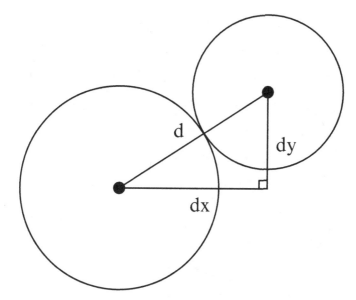

Fig. 7.32: A right triangle is found in between the two marbles in a collision

Axis of Collision

Two marbles of unequal size are shown colliding in Fig. 7.32. The axis of collision is defined by (dx, dy) and its direction depends on the order of the subtraction,
as shown in Code Listing 7.17. The distance d is calculated as R was previously and
is used to modify the *vector* $\langle dx, dy \rangle$ to be a *unit vector* $\langle dx/d, dy/d \rangle$ instead.

Code Listing 7.17: Axis of collision. Direction depends on the order of subtraction

```
#
# toward marble #1
#
dx1 = x1 - x2
dy1 = y1 - y2
#
# toward marble #2
#
dx2 = x2 - x1
dy2 = y2 - y1
#
```

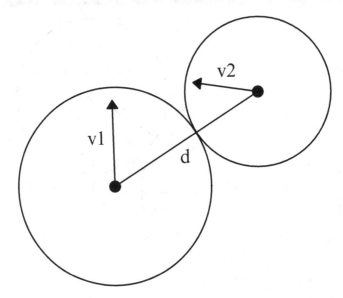

Fig. 7.33: Rotation by Theta. We need to write velocity v in terms of u and w

Rotation by Theta

We need to write velocity v in terms of u and w. Dividing dx and dy by distance d means that $dx = \cos(\theta)$ and $dy = \sin(\theta)$. Since the axis of collision is (dx, dy) the direction perpendicular to the axis of collision, used to calculate w, is $(-dy, dx)$.

$$\begin{pmatrix} u \\ w \end{pmatrix} = \begin{pmatrix} dx & dy \\ -dy & dx \end{pmatrix} \begin{pmatrix} v_x \\ v_y \end{pmatrix}$$

After changing the u value we will rebuild our new v by rotating "back" in the opposite direction $-\theta$. This rotation is done by transposing* matrix entries across the diagonal. We use a *dot product* in our actual code to simplify the arithmetic.

$$\begin{pmatrix} v_x \\ v_y \end{pmatrix} = \begin{pmatrix} dx & -dy \\ dy & dx \end{pmatrix} \begin{pmatrix} u \\ w \end{pmatrix}$$

---

* See, for instance: R. Charles et al., *Algebra 2*. Prentice Hall, 2012.

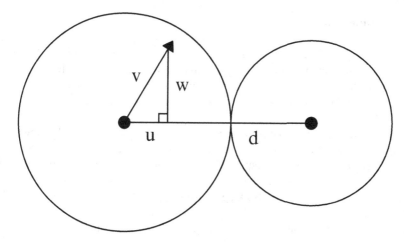

Fig. 7.34: Collision rotated. The distance d is shown here only for reference

Dot Product

The collision shown in Fig. 7.33 has been rotated by θ as shown in Fig. 7.34, and the velocity v is now written in terms of u and w rather than v_x and v_y.

$$u = \quad dx \cdot v_x + dy \cdot v_y$$
$$w = -dy \cdot v_x + dx \cdot v_y$$

These two dot products perform our rotation without the angle θ appearing directly in either calculation. Changes to u happen as in the 1-D case and then...

$$v_x = \quad dx \cdot u - dy \cdot w$$
$$v_y = \quad dy \cdot u + dx \cdot w$$

... two more dot products, with the entries transposed across the diagonal, rebuild v.

Lab734: Blue Marble

Code Listings 7.18 and 7.19 show changes to both the Marble class and the main program in order to implement collisions between two marbles.

The one change to the main program is minor. Instead of turning lights off or on we instead call the new function for marbles that changes their velocities as a result of the collision.

The new marble function calculates the axis of collision as previously shown and then rewrites the velocity of both marbles in terms of u and w. The u values are changed (since the masses are equal this is a simple swap) and the new velocities are built. The dot product calculations shown previously are used to convert from v_x and v_y to u and w, then also back again from u and w to v_x and v_y. Of course the value of u is changed in between those two conversions.

Figure 7.35 shows planet Earth, which often collides with small celestial objects.

Fig. 7.35: Earth on 6 July 2015, not the 1972 photograph. Image courtesy of NASA

Code Listing 7.18: Addition to the Marble class

```
#
class Marble:
    #
    ...
    #
    def bounce(self,the_other_marble):
        #
        dx=self.x-the_other_marble.x
        dy=self.y-the_other_marble.y
        #
        d = sqrt(dx*dx + dy*dy)
        #
        dx/=d
        dy/=d
        #
        u1 =  dx*self.vx + dy*self.vy
        w1 = -dy*self.vx + dx*self.vy
        #
        u2 = ...
        w2 = ...
        #
        if u1>u2: return # moving apart
        #
        u1,u2 = u2,u1     # simple swap
        #
        self.vx = dx*u1 - dy*w1
        self.vy = dy*u1 + dx*w1
        #
        the_other_marble.vx = ...
        the_other_marble.vy = ...
        #
```

Code Listing 7.19: Change to the main program

```
#
def tick():
    #
    ...
    #
    # handshake problem
    #
    # if collision then bounce
    #
```

Obstacles

Code Listings 7.20 and 7.21 show changes to both the main program and the Marble class that implement collisions between marbles and an obstacle. The obstacle is a Marble object but it is not in the list of marbles. Instead, its size and position are set independently, and its velocity is set to zero.

As shown in Fig. 7.36 the obstacle does not move. It acts in the same manner as the other walls but depending on where a marble hits it the axis of collision could be in any direction. For this example the objects could be initialized at random in such a way that no collisions were occurring at time zero, at the start of the animation. However, in other scenarios that approach may not be as straightforward.

One general initialization technique that prevents immediate overlap begins by placing the larger objects first. (They will always be the most difficult to place last.) Then, for each new object that is placed, check if its initial position involves a collision with any other object that has already been placed and, if so, pick a different place to put the new one. Even if these placements are made at random they can be done in a loop that continues until an acceptable position is located.

Compare this issue to a similar one seen earlier in Lab414. Of course, in either case we may be attempting to fit more "stuff" into a particular space than is even possible, in which case we need to find more space!

Code Listing 7.20: Additions to the main program

```
#
obstacle=Marble(cnvs)
#
obstacle.r  = 50.0
obstacle.x  =  w/2
obstacle.y  =  h/2
obstacle.vx =  0.0
obstacle.vy =  0.0
obstacle.lightOn()
#
def tick():
    #
    for marble in marbles:
        #
        if obstacle.collide(marble):
            #
            obstacle.bounceWall(marble)
            #
        #
    #
    ...
    #
```

Code Listing 7.21: Addition to the Marble class

```
#
class Marble:
    #
    ...
    #
    def bounceWall(self,the_other_marble):
        #
        # self is the obstacle
        #
        # axis of collision is toward the obstacle
        #
        #
        if u<0: return # moving away from obstacle
        #
        u *= -1.0        # bounce like it hit a wall
        #
        the_other_marble.vx = dx*u - dy*w
        the_other_marble.vy = dy*u + dx*w
        #
```

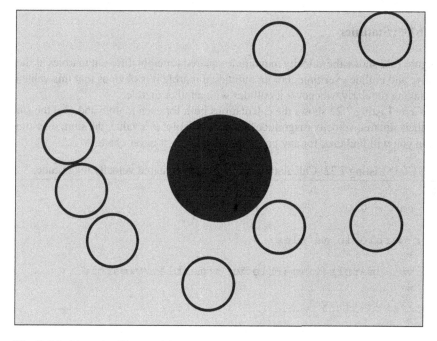

Fig. 7.36: Obstacle. The marbles behave as always but the obstacle never moves

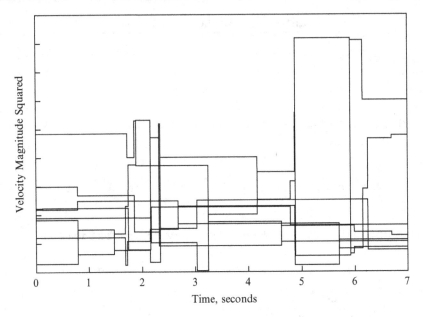

Fig. 7.37: Velocity magnitude squared. Eight marbles are tracked over time

Lab735: Statistics

Figure 7.37 shows the velocity magnitude squared for eight different marbles as they move and collide over time. For an individual marble it is obvious that this value is changing regularly, whenever it collides with another marble.

Code Listing 7.22 shows the calculations both for each marble and also the sum of their squared velocity magnitudes. Now if you plot *this* value, the sum, over time then you will find that, for any particular animation, it never changes.

Code Listing 7.22: Calculating the sum of the squared velocity magnitudes

```
#
vv_sum = 0.0
#
for marble in marbles:
    #
    vv = marble.vx*marble.vx + marble.vy*marble.vy
    #
    vv_sum += vv
    #
#
```

Chapter 8
Modeling, Part II

8.1 Herd Dynamics

We modify our Marble class to include turning, sensing, and intention.

These are all forms of animal behavior and so we call the objects antelopes, as shown in Fig. 8.1. Importantly, we will observe large-scale global properties emerge from small-scale local characteristics.

The *ANTALOPE.*

Fig. 8.1: Antelope. Woodcut by Edward Topsell, London, 1658 (Image courtesy of Special Collections, University of Houston Libraries)

© Springer International Publishing 2016
S. Torbert, *Applied Computer Science*, DOI 10.1007/978-3-319-30866-1_8

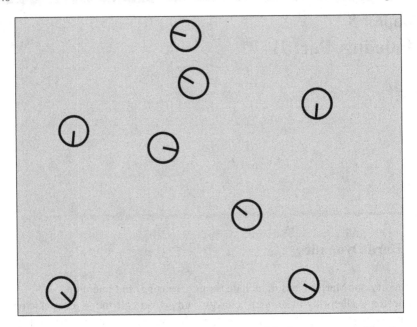

Fig. 8.2: Herd of Antelopes. The internal "arrow" indicates current direction

Lab811: Counterclockwise

Figure 8.2 shows a herd of antelopes moving in *almost* the same manner as a list of marbles. However, in addition to colliding with each other and bouncing off walls, an antelope also has a sense of its own direction.

At each time step an antelope changes its heading by turning counterclockwise as indicated by the "arrow" drawn within each outline-only circle.

Code Listings 8.1 and 8.2 show the first of many differences between a Marble class and an Antelope class. The new function for turning uses the four formulas shown previously for right triangles, and our main program now has them turn whenever they move.

$$x = R\cos\theta$$
$$y = R\sin\theta$$

$$R = \sqrt{x^2 + y^2}$$
$$\theta = \arctan(y, x)$$

Code Listing 8.1: From a Marble class to an Antelope class

```
#
class Antelope:
    #
    ...
    #
    def turn_me(self):
        #
        # deconstruct velocity
        #
        theta = atan2(self.vy, self.vx )
        speed = sqrt( self.vx*self.vx + \
                      self.vy*self.vy )
        #
        # change angle... counterclockwise
        #
        theta -= 0.1 * pi/180.0
        #
        # reconstruct velocity
        #
        self.vx = speed*cos(theta)
        self.vy = speed*sin(theta)
    #
```

Code Listing 8.2: Main program. Antelopes move like marbles but also turn

```
#
def tick():
    #
    ...
    #
    for antelope in antelopes:
        #
        antelope.turn_me()
        #
        antelope.move_me(dt)
        #
    #
    #
    # handshake problem
    #
    # if collision then bounce
    #
```

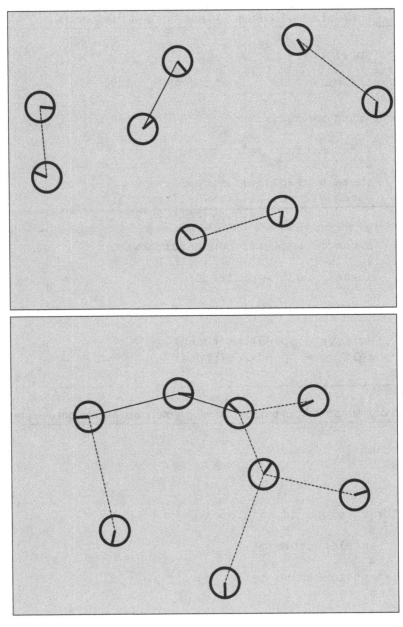

Fig. 8.3: Nearest neighbors. Each antelope calculates the distance between itself and every other antelope. Then, a line is drawn to whichever of its neighbors was found at the minimum distance. Since the herd is dynamic many variations are possible. *Top*: Complete segmentation into pairs. *Bottom*: A single cluster with two hubs

Lab812: Nearest Neighbors

Figure 8.3 shows our same herd of antelopes but now with each nearest neighbor indicated by a line. Code Listing 8.3 suggests how to determine who the nearest neighbor is for a particular antelope object.

We find the distances in the same manner as when we check for a collision but in addition keep track of which neighbor has had the minimum distance *so far* and also what that smallest distance was. Then, as each distance is calculated we can compare it to see if this one is in fact smaller than what we *had* thought was the smallest. If so, we update our nearest neighbor tracking information.

After we repeat these checks and updates, comparing each antelope in the herd, then whoever we think our nearest neighbor is *really is* our nearest neighbor because we have checked them all. The same loop works the same way for each antelope and, in general, you may not be the nearest neighbor of your nearest neighbor.

Observe that we are now *aware of* but still not *reacting to* our nearest neighbor. Even the relative headings of a pair of nearest neighbors may be in completely opposite directions. As with constellations of stars, over time they will drift apart.

Next we will keep the antelopes close together by having them exert an actual influence on each other.

Code Listing 8.3: Drawing lines to each antelope's nearest neighbor

```
#
def tick():
    #
    ...
    #
    # handshake problem
    #
    # check the distance between each pair
    #
    # antelopes track the minimum distance
    # between themselves and all others
    #
    # update the minimum distance, and the
    # neighbor, as smaller ones are found
    #
    #
    # afterward
    #
    # draw lines to the nearest neighbors
    #
#
```

Lab813: Clumping

Code Listing 8.4 shows a function similar to the one for turning but this one is for changing speed. The actual values used to slow down could be anything, or even passed as arguments to the function.

Antelopes are able to alter their own velocities in ways that marbles could not because animals respond not only to physical law but also to intentional change.

To move like one's nearest neighbor there are two steps. First, compare your speed with your neighbor's speed and compare your heading with their heading. Second, change your speed up or down (faster or slower) to more closely match your neighbor's speed, and turn left or turn right to more closely match their heading.

Examine the behavior of the nearest neighbors in Fig. 8.4. Not only are neighbors close together but their motion is also aligned. In fact, over time neighbors will not only stay together but drift closer, too.

An antelope's desire to act more like its nearest neighbor is fundamentally different from a marble colliding with another marble. For a collision the two objects must touch, whereas the influence of peer-imitation can happen at some distance.

Code Listing 8.4: Similar to the turning function but this one is for changing speed

```
#
class Antelope:
    #
    ...
    #
    def slow_down(self):
        #
        # deconstruct velocity
        #
        theta = atan2(self.vy,self.vx )
        speed = sqrt( self.vx*self.vx + \
                      self.vy*self.vy )
        #
        # change speed... slow down
        #
        speed -= 2.0               # ad hoc
        #
        if speed<5.0: speed=5.0  # floor
        #
        # reconstruct velocity
        #
        self.vx = speed*cos(theta)
        self.vy = speed*sin(theta)
    #
```

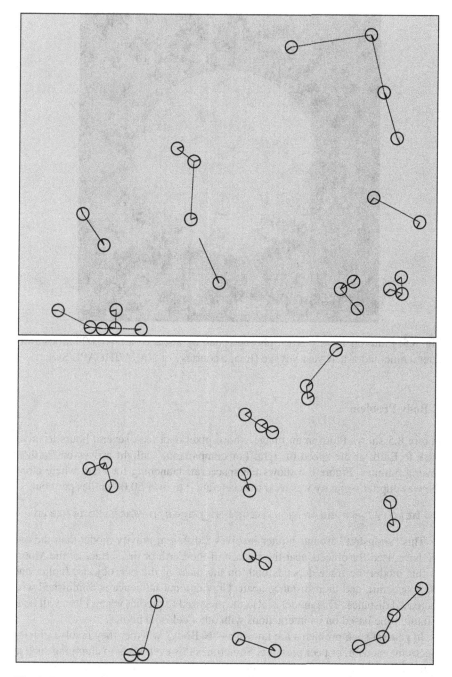

Fig. 8.4: Herd of antelopes. Groups of neighbors are obviously clumping together

Fig. 8.5: Pluto on 13 July 2015, photographed by a spacecraft 476,000 miles away after a nine-and-a-half year voyage (Image courtesy of NASA/JHUAPL/SwRI)

N-Body Problem

Figure 8.5 shows Pluto in an image whose pixel data took several hours to travel back to Earth at the speed of light. For comparison, sunlight arrives on Earth in several minutes. Figure 8.6 shows the spacecraft launching for Pluto where along the way Jupiter's gravity was used to accelerate it to over 50,000 miles per hour.

```
http://www.nasa.gov/mission_pages/newhorizons/main
```

This "slingshot" around Jupiter involves a different gravity model than the one we have used for objects near the surface of the Earth or the surface of the Moon. In this model the force depends both on the mass of the two objects, Jupiter and the spacecraft, and their distance apart. Gravitational influence is diminished with increased distance. This model is also the one used to predict where Pluto will be at a future time based on its interactions with other celestial bodies.

In general such problems are known as "N-Body" whether they involve gravity, electromagnetism, or peer pressure. Sometimes this even leads to clumping such as in the asteroid belt or rings of a planet, or as we have just seen with the neighbors of antelopes. Similarly we next examine the modeling of large crowds of pedestrians, a case whose size makes in-person on-site experiments prohibitively expensive.

Fig. 8.6: Trip to Pluto. *Top*: The gravity of Jupiter, shown here on 8 January 2007 with its volcanic moon Io alongside, accelerated the spacecraft to over 50,000 mph. For scale, Io is larger than Pluto and Jupiter's Great Red Spot is larger than Earth. Bottom: Launch on 19 January 2006 (Images courtesy of NASA/Johns Hopkins Applied Physics Laboratory/Southwest Research Institute and NASA)

Fig. 8.7: The National Mall on 20 January 2009 (Image courtesy of the U.S. Department of Defense, photo credit U.S. Air Force Senior Master Sgt. Thomas Meneguin)

Lab814: Profiling

Figures 8.7 and 8.8 show large crowds. Modeling a case of this size requires efficient code, and Code Listings 8.5 and 8.6 show how we can analyze runtime using a profiler. For instance, we might only check for collisions with a nearest neighbor. See also *On the Modeling of Pedestrian Motion* by Rainald Löhner.

Code Listing 8.5: Tick, written with functions in order to facilitate profiling

```
#
def tick():
    #
    find_nearest_neighbor()
    #
    collide_bounce_nbr()
    #
    change_velocity() # both speed and angle heading
    #
    cnvs.after(1,tick)
    #
```

Fig. 8.8: Times Square on 14 August 1945 (Image courtesy of the New York World-Telegram and the Sun Newspaper Photograph Collection, Library of Congress Prints and Photographs Division, photo credit Dick DeMarsico)

Code Listing 8.6: Results, run with the "python -m cProfile Lab814.py" option

```
  calls      time   function
   8153    13.815   Lab814.py:58(find_nearest_neighbor)
5479913     8.343   {math.sqrt}
 587016     4.811   Tkinter.py:2257(coords)
   8153     3.486   Lab814.py:97(change_velocity)
 195672     3.414   antelope.py:39(move_me)
 195672     1.905   antelope.py:89(speed)
 195672     1.898   antelope.py:71(turn_me)
 978384     1.762   {math.atan2}
 587040     1.045   {math.cos}
 587040     0.975   {math.sin}
 195672     0.766   antelope.py:111(collide)
   8153     0.486   Lab814.py:40(collide_bounce_nbr)
   8153     0.136   Lab814.py:137(tick)
    544     0.004   antelope.py:129(bounce)
     24     0.001   antelope.py:7(__init__)
```

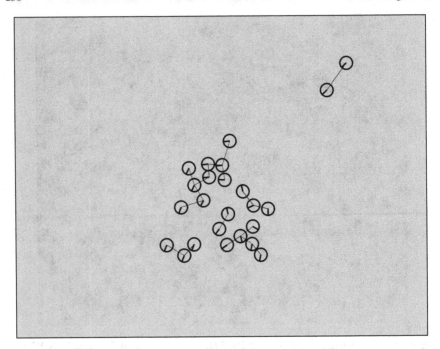

Fig. 8.9: Herd of antelopes, swarming. Each antelope turns toward the middle

Lab815: Swarming

Figure 8.9 shows the result of antelopes who not only intend to behave more like their nearest neighbors but are also trying to turn toward the middle of the screen.

The turn toward the middle involves a change to the angle θ that is only half as large as the turn toward the nearest neighbor's heading. In this way, if the two goals are in conflict then the secondary goal will diminish the primary goal but not eliminate it. On the other hand, if the two goals are in concert then the antelope will turn in an exaggerated fashion toward the agreed-upon direction.

These two straightforward local actions give rise to a stark global phenomena which emerges naturally and without the need for widespread direct orchestration.

Similar models may be constructed which account for the presence of various obstacles. In addition to bouncing off the wall of an obstacle, as we saw with marbles, the placement of the obstacles also restricts an antelope's vision. A nearby antelope who is obstructed from view will thus not be identified as a nearest neighbor.

By using smaller circles as obstacles, and also placing many of them close together, arbitrary shapes can be produced. A corridor might consist of many hundreds of circles lined up to form walls and doorways. Any number of herd-level tasks can then be studied, such as maze escaping or (similarly) evacuation.

8.2 Predator-Prey

Imagine two types of animals, one predator and the other prey. We begin with only the prey, which we will call "rabbits," and later add the predator, called "wolves."

For simplicity we model rabbits that move in discrete chunks on a grid, or lattice. At each step a rabbit moves but not with the free-range of an antelope or a marble. Instead each rabbit always moves exactly by a distance of $2r$ and in one of only four directions: up, down, left, right.

Think about which of our previous classes is best suited to use as a starting point for the Rabbit class. If as you make progress it seems that a different choice would have been better then stop, save a backup copy of all your work, and begin your code again from the other perspective.

Do not continue down a path you believe to be flawed when an alternative approach, which you believe to be more promising, is available. The code you wrote yesterday is done but the code you write today, and tomorrow, is yours to create in whatever manner you see fit.

Lab821: Single Rabbit

Code Listings 8.7 and 8.8 get you started on the lonely rabbit simulation shown in Fig. 8.10. What happens when a rabbit moves to the edge of the screen? Does it bounce off a wall? Or wrap around to the other side? Or does it matter?

Code Listing 8.7: Defining a rabbit object, filename: `rabbit.py`

```
#
class Rabbit:
    #
    def __init__(self,cnvs):
        #
        self.hungry=False
        #
    #
    def mark_as_hungry(self):
        #
        self.hungry=True
        #
    #
    def check_is_hungry(self):
        #
        return self.hungry
        #
    #
#
```

Fig. 8.10: A lonely rabbit stuck on a lattice: up, down, left, right

Code Listing 8.8: A list of rabbits but with only one object, for now

```
#
from rabbit import Rabbit
#
rabbits=[]
#
def tick():
    #
    ...
    #
#
rabbits.append( Rabbit(cnvs) )
#
```

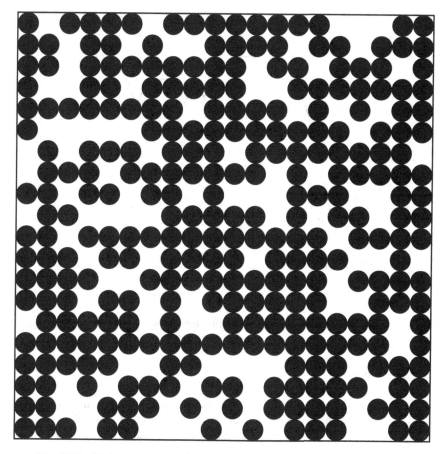

Fig. 8.11: Observed results, exponential growth in the rabbit population

Lab822: Breeding Rabbits

A lonely rabbit no more. Code Listing 8.9 uses an unnatural breeding mechanism but the real questions is, Do the observed results in Fig. 8.11 match nature or not?

Code Listing 8.9: Breeding rabbits but with an artificial limit imposed

```
n=len(rabbits)
j=0
while j<n and len(rabbits)<1000:
    #
    rabbits.append( Rabbit(cnvs) ) # breed
    j+=1
```

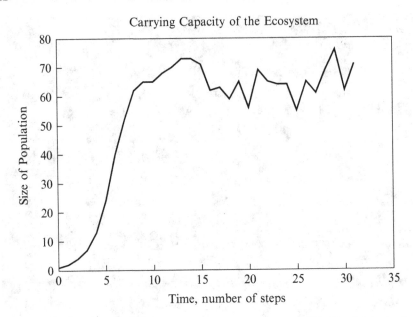

Fig. 8.12: Carrying capacity, the initial population boom levels off quickly: logistic

Lab823: Hunger

A less artificial mechanism for controlling population growth is to model the competition for food as shown in Code Listings 8.10 and 8.11. If two rabbits are close enough together then one will get hungry (at random) because there is only so much food to eat. Figures 8.12 and 8.13 show the results, a better match than before.

Code Listing 8.10: Handshake problem, one group: rabbits

```
j=0
while j<len(rabbits):
    #
    k=j+1
    while k<len(rabbits):
        #
        if rabbits[j].collide(rabbits[k]):
            if ...
                rabbits[j].mark_as_hungry()
            else:
                rabbits[k].mark_as_hungry()
        ...
```

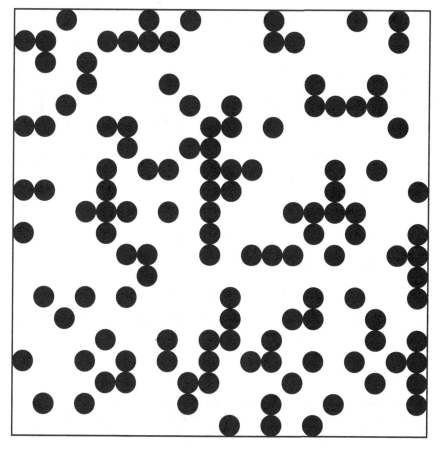

Fig. 8.13: Competition for food, some neighboring rabbits are about to go hungry

Code Listing 8.11: Looping backward, again, so as not to skip over any rabbits

```
j=len(rabbits)-1
#
while j>=0:
    #
    if rabbits[j].check_is_hungry():
        #
        rabbits[j].delete_me()           # die/starve
        rabbits.pop(j)
    else:
        #
        rabbits[j].move_me()             # move
    ...
```

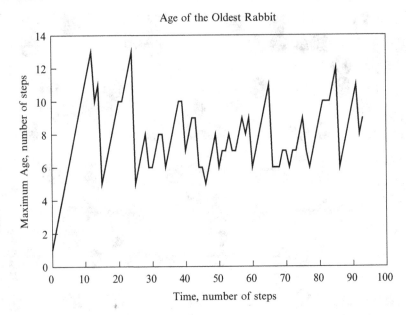

Fig. 8.14: Maximum age, how old is the oldest rabbit? Unfortunately not very old

Lab824: Age Distribution

For an agent-based model to accurately represent a real animal, society, or phenomena, our code will need to include more individual characteristics that distinguish the agents. Code Listing 8.12 shows how age might be modeled by the Rabbit class.

Figure 8.14 reports the age of the oldest rabbit over time and Fig. 8.15 shows a snapshot of age distribution at step 13 (70 total rabbits) and step 32 (62 rabbits).

Code Listing 8.12: Each rabbit tracks their own age, and grows older

```
#
def __init__(self,cnvs):
    #
    self.age=0
    #
#
def move_me(self):
    #
    self.age+=1
    #
#
```

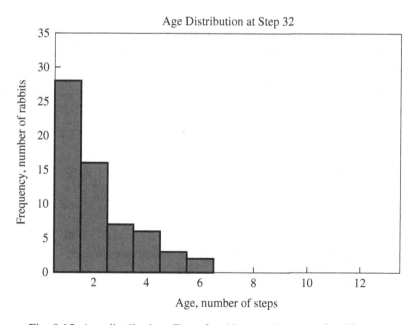

Fig. 8.15: Age distribution. *Top*: after 13 steps. *Bottom*: after 32 steps

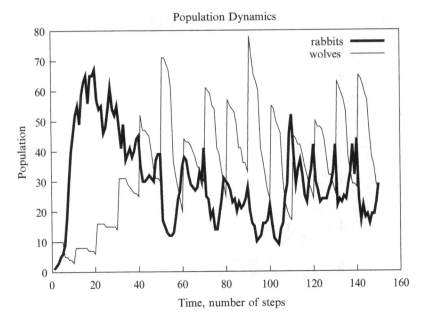

Fig. 8.16: Population dynamics, rabbits and wolves alternate from peak to valley

Lab825: Wolves

Code Listing 8.13 shows a wolf always winning the "coin flip" but needing food every four steps or it dies of hunger itself. Wolves have two offspring exactly once at age ten. Results are shown in Figs. 8.16 and 8.17. Since the underlying parameters all are ad hoc you may tune them as you see fit, just be prepared for major changes.

Code Listing 8.13: Handshake problem, two groups: wolves and rabbits

```
shuffle(wolves)
for wolf in wolves:
    #
    j=len(rabbits)-1
    while j>=0:
        if wolf.collide(rabbits[j]):
            #
            rabbits[j].delete_me()      # die/eaten
            rabbits.pop(j)
            #
            wolf.reset_hunger()
        ...
```

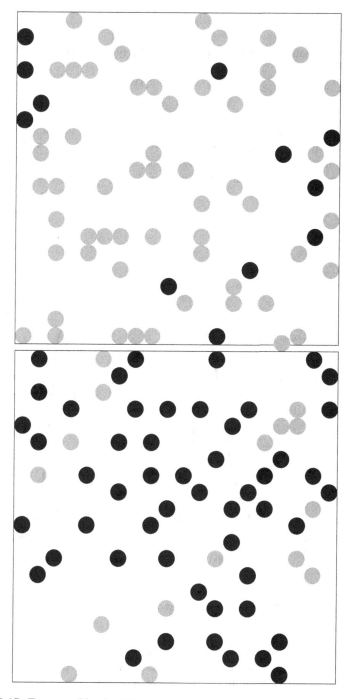

Fig. 8.17: *Top*: step 55, 12 rabbits and 61 wolves. *Bottom*: step 110, 52 and 17

Analytic Model

A purely mathematical model can also describe our two interacting populations:

$$dx = c_1x - c_2xy$$
$$dy = -c_3y + c_4xy$$

At each step the changes are calculated from the current population sizes and then each population size is updated. Obviously this is a coupled system with each variable depending on the other variable's value, too.

As shown in Fig. 8.18 we call x the rabbits and y the wolves, using:

$c_1 = 4.00$
$c_2 = 1.00$
$c_3 = 2.00$
$c_4 = 0.25$

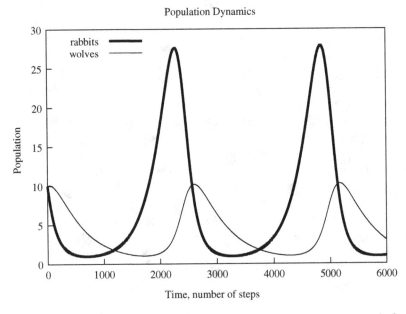

Fig. 8.18: Population dynamics, rabbits and wolves alternating but not as before

Additional investigations may include social networks, seasons (agents interacting with their environment), migration, commerce, clans or tribes, and even physical characteristics such as strength, speed, and eyesight, along with a genetic blend of parental "chromosomes" among their offspring.

8.3 Bioinformatics

Butyrylcholinesterase is an enzyme encoded by the BCHE gene. Gene sequence data is available from the National Center for Biotechnology Information at:

http://www.ncbi.nlm.nih.gov

The eleven animals considered in this chapter all have BCHE gene sequences of length $O(1800)$ characters. In fact most are the exact same length, some are off by only three, and one (chimpanzee) differs by $O(100)$.

We want to build a Tree of Life based on the similarity of these gene sequences. This is not a full alignment of an entire genome as much longer sequences would be needed for that. (And better algorithms, and bigger computers.) Also, our investigation uses the Levenshtein distance for pairwise comparisons rather than the more customizable Needleman-Wunsch method.

In addition, we do not convert similarity scores between genes into evolutionary distance and, for building the actual tree, we suggest a so-called "greedy" algorithm rather than a more sophisticated neighbor-join that might minimize total branch length. Our goal is only to present a broad introduction of alignment issues and similarity measures, and to show the kinds of results one can achieve.

Lab831: Similarity of Two Words

The Levenshtein distance finds the total number of edits necessary to transform from one word to another. Consider first the case where two words have the same length and just count the total differences. Code Listing 8.14 shows a few test cases.

Code Listing 8.14: A few test cases, counting the number of different letters

```
Word #1:   cortex
Word #2:   vortex
Number of letters different:   1

Word #1:   branch
Word #2:   trance
Number of letters different:   2

Word #1:   kittens
Word #2:   kitchen
Number of letters different:   4

Word #1:   apples
Word #2:   oranges
Word lengths do not match!
```

Lab832: A Single Gap

If the lengths differ by one then we can use a loop to find where in the shorter word
we should insert a "gap" for the best possible match. Code Listing 8.15 shows two
examples where only the best placement of the gap is reported and the associated
number is the sum of the difference count and the number of gaps.

Code Listing 8.15: Two examples of inserting a single gap with a loop

```
kitchen
kit-ten
2
cart
ca-t
1
```

Lab833: Multiple Gaps

Code Listing 8.16 recursively places multiple gaps and Code Listing 8.17 reports
partial results of the corresponding search for a best match.

Code Listing 8.16: Recursive placement of gaps, all possibilities

```
#
def recur(word1,word2,j,chlist,gaps,maxgaps):
    #
    if len(chlist)==len(word1):
        ...
    else:
        #
        # try inserting a gap in this slot
        #
        if gaps<maxgaps:
            recur(word1 ,word2                ,\
                  j        ,chlist+['-']       ,\
                  gaps+1,maxgaps                )
        #
        # try inserting the actual letter
        #
        if j<len(word2):
            recur(word1 ,word2                , \
                  j+1    ,chlist+[word2[j]], \
                  gaps   ,maxgaps                )
    #
```

Code Listing 8.17: Trying all possible arrangements. Looking for the best match

```
    :
anagrams
al-a-rms
5
anagrams
al-ar-ms
4
anagrams
al-arm-s
5
anagrams
al-arms-
6
anagrams
ala--rms
4
anagrams # best
ala-r-ms
3
anagrams
ala-rm-s
4
anagrams
ala-rms-
5
anagrams
alar--ms
4
anagrams
alar-m-s
5
anagrams
alar-ms-
6
anagrams
alarm--s
5
anagrams
alarm-s-
6
anagrams
alarms--
6
```

Lab834: Enzyme DNA

We naively apply the previous technique to our BCHE gene sequences, where only
the difference count is required if we stay within the following same-length groups:

- human, tiger, cat, dog, cattle, horse, orangutan
- mouse, chicken

Code Listing 8.18: Which pair of sequences has the closest similarity measure?

```
File #1:   bengal_tiger
File #2:   domestic_cat
Number of letters different:   12

File #1:   human
File #2:   domestic_cat
Number of letters different:   191

File #1:   cattle
File #2:   domestic_cat
Number of letters different:   173

File #1:   human
File #2:   cattle
Number of letters different:   178

File #1:   dog
File #2:   domestic_cat
Number of letters different:   109

File #1:   dog
File #2:   bengal_tiger
Number of letters different:   115

File #1:   sumatran_orangutan
File #2:   cattle
Number of letters different:   173

File #1:   sumatran_orangutan
File #2:   human
Number of letters different:   23
----------------------------------------
File #1:   house_mouse
File #2:   chicken
Number of letters different:   1336
```

Dynamic Programming

Even though the lengths of the cattle and chicken sequences are off by only three there are still $O\left(10^9\right)$ possibilities for the placement of gaps. A faster way to make these comparisons is dynamic programming as outlined in Code Listing 8.19.

Code Listing 8.19: Dynamic programming as an alternative to recursive search

```
#
def levenshtein_distance(gene1,gene2):
    #
    dp=[0]*(m*n)      # m rows, n columns
    #
    # loop across the top row
        dp[0*n+j]=j
    #
    # loop down the left column
        dp[k*n+0]=k
    #
    # loop j=1,2,...,n-1
        # loop k=1,2,...,m-1
            #
            if gene1[j-1]==gene2[k-1]:
                dp[k*n+j]=dp[(k-1)*n+(j-1)]  # match
            #
            else:
                #
                # gap in gene1
                #
                opt1=dp[(k  )*n+(j-1)]+1
                #
                # gap in gene2
                #
                opt2=dp[(k-1)*n+(j  )]+1
                #
                # count difference
                #
                opt3=dp[(k-1)*n+(j-1)]+1
                #
                # principal of optimality
                #
                dp[k*n+j]=min(opt1,min(opt2,opt3))
            #
    return dp[-1]
#
```

Code Listing 8.20: All pairs Levenshtein distance similarity results

```
 0  bengal_tiger
 1  domestic_cat
 2  dog
 3  cattle
 4  horse
 5  human
 6  sumatran_orangutan
 7  house_mouse
 8  norway_rat
 9  chimpanzee
10  chicken
```

	1	2	3	4	5	6	7	8	9	10
0	12	115	176	149	195	187	330	331	306	478
1		109	172	144	190	182	324	322	301	477
2			192	162	193	183	335	335	303	492
3				154	175	170	341	337	282	468
4					172	168	332	331	281	473
5						23	348	337	132	471
6							343	329	148	464
7								137	445	509
8									455	513
9										566

Lab835: All Pairs Comparison

Code Listing 8.20 shows results for the BCHE gene, where a smaller score means more similar, and Code Listing 8.21 outlines the code in our main program.

Code Listing 8.21: Handshake problem, one group: BCHE gene sequences

```
#
filenames=open('list_of_files.txt','r').read().split()
j=0
while j<len(filenames):
    #
    gene1=open(filenames[j]+'.txt','r').read().strip()
    #
    k=j+1
    while k<len(filenames):
        ...
        result=levenshtein_distance(gene1,gene2)
#
```

Tree of Life

Using these similarity results we can now build a Tree of Life.

Note how our dynamic programming code may insert gaps even if the sequence lengths are equal, in order to find a closer match. Thus the similarity of mouse and chicken is 509 and not 1336, for instance. Likewise for "kittens" and "kitchen" we find "kit-tens" and "kitchen-" with a score of 3, better than a straight difference count based on equal lengths previously reported as 4.

Algorithm 8.3.1 outlines our tree building procedure. At each step we find the pair with the best similarity score. That pair is combined into a single "node" and all other scores involving the pair are replaced with their average.

Algorithm 8.3.1 Using the Levenshtein distance to build a Tree of Life

---

```
 1: while j = 0, 1, 2, ... do
 2:     while k = j + 1, j + 2, ... do
 3:         score[j, k] = levenshtein
 4:     end while
 5: end while
 6: while t = 2 → len(list) do
 7:     pair[j, k] = min(score)
 8:     while i = not(j, k) do
 9:         score[i, pair] = (score[i, j] + score[i, k])/2
10:         delete(score[i, j])
11:         delete(score[i, k])
12:     end while
13: end while
14: draw(tree)
```

For example, tiger and cat have the best similarity score (12) so they are paired together first. Then, all other scores involving tiger or cat are replaced with an average from the two. Eventually we will also pair together pairs rather than individuals but the same rules apply. The process continues:

- tiger and cat
- human and orangutan
- dog and tiger/cat
- mouse and rat
- chimpanzee and human/orangutan
- ...
- ALL and chicken

It should not be surprising that chicken is matched last since it is the only non-mammal in the list. Code Listing 8.22 on the following page shows our final result.

Code Listing 8.22: Tree of Life based on the BCHE gene

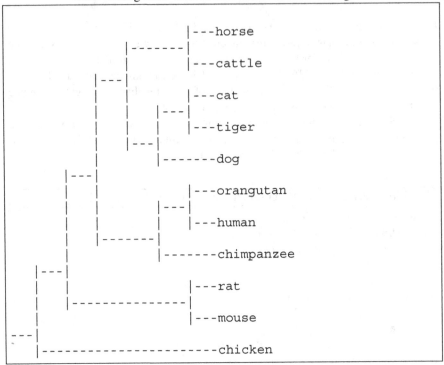

Achievement

Despite our remarkable genetic similarities it remains quite obvious, as Fig. 8.19 documents, that only humans have yet managed to photograph a sunset—on Mars.

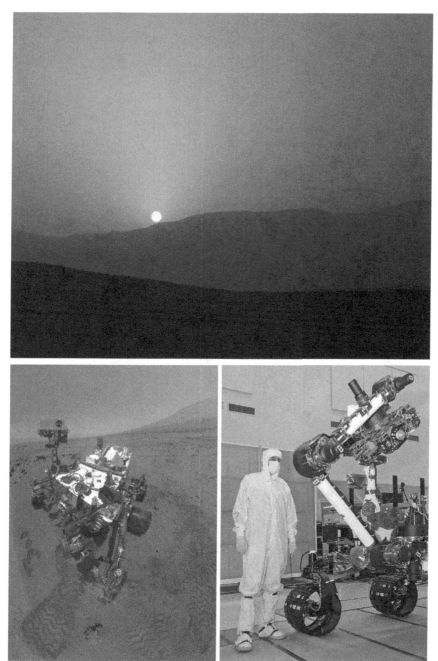

Fig. 8.19: *Curiosity* rover. *Top*: Martian sunset. *Bottom left*: Self-portrait on Mars. *Right*: Preparations on Earth (Images courtesy of NASA/JPL-Caltech/Malin Space Science Systems/Texas A&M, NASA/JPL-Caltech/MSSS, and NASA/JPL-Caltech)

Postscript

I wrote this book while on a sabbatical from Thomas Jefferson High School for Science and Technology where I have taught Computer Science since 2001.

I am fortunate to have worked in the Computer Systems Lab at TJ since 2004 and this past year in the Center for Computational Fluid Dynamics at George Mason University. I owe more than I could ever repay to both of these places.

This book is designed to speak to a wide and varied audience. News related to high school and undergraduate participation in Computer Science has become grim in recent years. Efforts are underway to change those trends and over time I believe the field will grow. I have myself been writing courses since 2003 and this book is my view on how best to present CS to beginning students.

I hope you find something here to grab hold of, something to spark your interest, something even that takes your breath away.

Fairfax, Virginia   Shane Torbert
August 2011

© Springer International Publishing 2016   279
S. Torbert, *Applied Computer Science*, DOI 10.1007/978-3-319-30866-1

Printed in the United States
By Bookmasters